"Born out of more than twer ministry, Donna Eschenauer's *First Communion Liturgies* is a compendium of wise pastoral suggestions rooted in real-life experiences. Collaborative to the core, in an era when individualism too often triumphs, Eschenauer envisions celebrations that are integral to parish life, celebrated in the midst of the gathered assembly and formative for child, family, and parish. Assuming the Rite of Christian Initiation of Adults and the Third Edition of the Roman Missal as foundational, Eschenauer handles thorny questions with wisdom and grace, incorporating stories drawn from her rich experience of pastoral ministry. Intended to be read as a whole, Eschenauer's *First Communion Liturgies* is rich in theology without being pedantic, loaded with fine pastoral suggestions that proved successful, and enhanced by references and recommendations to other resources."

—Dr. Julia Upton, RSM
Distinguished Professor of Theology
St. John's University, New York

"This is a very positive and promising work—the enthusiasm of the author for the subject is contagious! The many practical suggestions—along with the clear grasp of the background material, and a pleasant writing style, have all contributed to make this a very encouraging and inspiring 'read' for me."

—Rev. Joseph C. Henchey, CSS
Professor of Dogmatic Theology
St. Joseph's Seminary, New York

First Communion Liturgies

Preparing First-Class First Celebrations

Donna M. Eschenauer

LITURGICAL PRESS

Collegeville, Minnesota

www.litpress.org

1	2	3	4	5	6	7	8	9

Library of Congress Cataloging-in-Publication Data

Eschenauer, Donna.
　　First communion liturgies : preparing first-class first celebrations / Donna Eschenauer.
　　　pages cm
　　ISBN 978-0-8146-4967-1 — ISBN 978-0-8146-4992-3 (ebook)
　　1. First communion—Catholic Church.　2. Catholic Church—Liturgy. I.Title.

BX2237.E83　2014
264'.02036—dc23　　　　　　　　　　　　　　　　　　　2014008775

To all the children and families
who have motivated my passion for best liturgical practices
for the celebration of First Communion

To all of my teachers and colleagues
who support a vision that has enabled me
to teach, research, write, and practice in a manner
that serves the church well

To my family
who inspires me daily to continue the conversation
toward Traditioning at its best

Contents

Introduction

The sacramental character of faith finds its highest expression in the Eucharist. The Eucharist is a precious nourishment for faith: an encounter with Christ truly present in the supreme act of his love, the life-giving gift of himself.

—Pope Francis, *Lumen Fidei* 44

We are a eucharistic people, and the celebration of the Eucharist reveals, in a unique way, the foundation for what it means to be human. The essence of the Eucharist embodies a profound sense of faith, hope, and love that holds within it the promise to transform the human heart and mind. Ultimately, this highest form of prayer reveals for us wisdom for everyday living and dying. The act of receiving Communion is an action of faith in the presence of God.

This is a book about First Communion liturgies. It is written out of deep concern and love for how we celebrate liturgy with children in the Roman Catholic Church. This interest is influenced by over twenty years of pastoral experience and practice in teaching and preparing the liturgy for First Communion. During that time, my colleagues and I worked passionately to establish celebrations of First Communion that remained consistent with a normative vision for liturgy. Our aim was always to remain true to the prayer of the church and never sell out to any form of entertainment. In this same regard, I invite you to consider a liturgical point of view for First Communion.

Experience shows that implementation of good liturgical practice for the celebration of First Communion requires the collaboration of pastors, religious educators, liturgists, and pastoral musicians. In addition, the education of parents, children, as well as the entire parish, is highly effective.

The celebration of First Communion is a moment of great joy, not only for the child and his or her family, but also for the entire parish. Therefore, it ought to be celebrated in the midst of the gathered community of faith. In other words, First Communion liturgies, at best, are an integral part of the liturgical life of the parish.

The pages that follow are written to read as a whole, not in isolation. Each chapter offers sound theology and practical pastoral suggestions for making the experience of First Communion prayerful and memorable, while at the same time in full conformity with the *General Instruction of the Roman Missal*, as well as other liturgical documents.

The overall purpose of *First Communion Liturgies* is to explore the practice of First Communion, uncover some of the pitfalls associated with it, and offer a practical resource for preparing celebrations that will enrich the lives of children and families, hence bringing them into a deeper relationship with God and the church.

The significance of this book rests in its assertion that maintains: ritual prayer is a formative experience that contributes to the religious development of the child. In general, therefore, if children are to develop awareness of the God who is active and present in all of life, we cannot afford to expose them to liturgy that fosters an eclipse of good liturgical principles. Rather, we must foster an atmosphere that highlights traditioning at its best, and good, prayerful liturgy is traditioning at its source and summit.

First Communion liturgies that move children toward "enchantment not entertainment"[1] are possible, especially when care and collaboration among pastors, priests, liturgists, musicians, parents, and religious educators is a regular, ongoing practice in the parish. This can be accomplished in a manner that benefits not only children and their families but also the entire parish community.

I propose that liturgies for First Communion honor the integrity of liturgical principles. This, in my view, is indispensable for the liturgical experience of those celebrating their First Communion. To better appreciate this proposal, *First Communion Liturgies* offers a reflective examination of one of the most important moments in the life of Catholic Christian children. In chapter 1 I look at the practice of liturgy with children. From there, chapter 2 gives a brief historical perspective of some of the developing patterns for celebrating First Communion through the centuries. Chapter 3 explores the theological context for the celebration of First Communion that serves as the foundation for good pastoral practice. Chapter 4 focuses on an educational process that will enhance the celebration of First Communion and beyond. Finally, based on scholarship and experience, chapter 5 offers practical pastoral ideas for preparing the liturgy for First Communion.

It has often been said that no one writes a book alone. I am very grateful to all those who teach me daily, especially Dr. Kieran Scott who teaches me to imagine that I can accomplish extraordinary things. I am grateful to my colleagues at St. Joseph's Seminary, particularly Msgr. Peter Vaccari and Fr. Kevin O'Reilly who provide great support as I respond to the vocation to write. Special thanks to those who graciously took the time to read this manuscript and offer many helpful suggestions, especially Paul Eschenauer, Cynthia Harrison, and Fr. Joseph Henchey, CSS. I am indebted to Barry Hudock and Andrew Edwards at Liturgical

Press. In addition to their gracious editorial guidance, I am extremely grateful for their interest in this work. Heartfelt thanks are owed to my family, especially my husband Paul, whose constant love and support I can always count on, especially when I am engrossed in research and writing. Last, to all the readers of this work, that you may be inspired by its thesis, and in turn, enhance First Communion liturgies.

1

Liturgy with Children

The child is the human being who is, right from the first, the partner of God.

—Karl Rahner[1]

The heart of the Roman Catholic faith is the celebration of the liturgy, particularly the Eucharist. This chapter takes into account the manner in which we celebrate liturgy with children. Critical to an appropriate approach to celebrating liturgy with children is insight into the religious imagination, the qualities of childhood, the *Directory of Masses with Children*, and the honored place of children within the assembly.

Liturgy and the Religious Imagination

Liturgy is an act of the imagination.[2] It therefore awakens the religious imagination and discloses rich meaning if we dare to leave the comfort zone of the rational and enter into the seemingly eclipsed, waiting arms of God's embrace. Undoubtedly, best liturgical practices speak to the religious imagination and offer a palpable sense of God's presence.

The church calls us to embrace the memory of Jesus Christ together with a hope-filled future spelled out through paschal mystery. This memory and hope is experienced and made real through liturgy, particularly in and through the Eucharist, which shows us how to live and how to die.

There is a link between the gift and grace of our imagination and the patterns of religious activity, particularly the practice of liturgy. "Imagination," writes Richard Cote, "can be described as the climate of faith, the condition of its possibility: neither its ground nor its goal of perfection, but a penultimate instrument of grace in a world whose final salvation remains an object of hope. And hope, as we know it, is always based on some promise and therefore on the ability to 'see' beyond what meets the eye. As St. Paul says, 'In hope we are saved. Now hope that is seen is not hope. For who hopes for what is seen?' (Romans 8:24). Hope, like faith, requires considerable imagination."[3]

Liturgical prayer, then, is the context for healing, shaping, and exercising the religious imaginative process. The pattern and structure of liturgy, that is, Word and sacrament, leads us to see what cannot be seen, and in the end, leads us to alternative realities. In other words, liturgy, the ritual prayer of the church, provides a way of seeing what might be. Through assembly, song, symbol, silence, and gesture, the message of the liturgy takes away all fear and passivity, awakening a new perspective and way of seeing the world. Seasoned in mystery, we can bathe in the presence of God through the images of ritual prayer. These, in turn, invite us to hope again. Unlocking the religious imagination is the hallmark of Christian maturity. The task of ministerial practice with children, then, is to nurture the religious imagination, or we risk mere reverberation.

In his work on religious development, Gabriel Moran writes, "The religious life of the small child is one of unending mystery and unalloyed wonder. The divine is everywhere, manifested in life's daily miracles."[4] That being said, children are natural mystics who have the natural capacity for wonder. Children are eager to learn and have a natural sense of God's greatness. Educational master Dwayne Huebner provides insight into the meaning of wonder. He writes, "Wonder has at least two meanings. Frequently we associate it with the feeling of doubt, curiosity, inquiry. We say 'I wonder if' or 'he wonders whether' and we associate with it such synonyms as speculate, conjecture, ponder, theorize, question, surmise, imagine. Certainly this is a common meaning, but I have in mind the other sense of the word. The meaning which is more clearly associated with such synonyms as astonishment, amazement, surprise, fascination, awe."[5]

I vividly remember two noteworthy moments from my own early childhood experience. One was while I was walking on the beach toward the beautiful, glistening cloud formations. I imagined I was walking straight toward God. The other occurred while sitting on a backyard swing with my mother. As I deliberately pinched the skin on my leg, I innocently asked, "What are people?" And I wondered why God made us. These childhood moments of wonder, I am convinced, launched my interest in theology.

Nurturing the religious imagination of children brings them closer to the sacred. Liturgy with children must reflect a profound sense of sacred time and have as its goal that all life is imbued with paschal mystery, the heart of Christian faith. And, as Mary Collins writes, "Anything less than a profound liturgical ministry for the young is a betrayal of trust, another form of exploitation of the young at their expense."[6]

Qualities of Childhood

Children capture for us the meaning of sensibility, playfulness, innocence, openness, directness, and vulnerability.[7]

Children are natural at play, wonder, surprise, and trust. Additionally, they have the profound ability to acquire greatness from simplicity. This calls to mind an experience I had with a nine-year-old child who went through the rites of Christian initiation. After the celebration of the Acceptance into the Order of Catechumens, where she experienced the signing of the senses, she exclaimed, "I felt like God was all over me." Clearly, this child experienced wonder in "participating with the time and being of the other."[8]

Distinctively, the understanding of what it means to be a child is essential for the practice of liturgy. Furthermore, an understanding of what it means to be childlike is essential for an understanding of adulthood.[9] The true meaning of adulthood discovered through the metaphor of the child essentially points us toward the mystery of what it means to be human. Significantly, Antoine de Saint-Exupéry writes in *The Little Prince*, "all grown-ups were once children— although few of them remember it."[10] Each of us, therefore, must come to liturgy with the disposition of a child. This point of view is crucial; for in and through the liturgy we enter a world of paradox, mystery, poetry, and symbol; in and through liturgy we are not independent; we are bound to one another through the common ritual of baptism. In baptism, and recaptured through Eucharist, we enter into relationship with Christ and the church. Children understand this better than anyone. Have you ever observed children on a playground? They welcome the "stranger," playing with all the inhabitants of that place without a care of their status in life; their only concern is that they are "little" people. The genuine worshipping community welcomes the stranger, and it exists to support its members in a gospel way of life.

Understandably, liturgy with children should not differ greatly from the Order of Mass because its purpose is to lead children toward celebrating with adults.[11] The way in which we prepare liturgy with children will impact a child's sense of God, church, and in the end, an understanding of full, active, and conscious participation in the prayer of the church.

In many ways, we need to bring people to the realization that liturgy is deeply connected to childhood; however, liturgy is never meant to be childish, entertaining, or a diversion from the complexities of life. Julia Upton reflects on the various obstacles to the church's vision of liturgy. One such obstacle, she notes, is unrealistic expectations, "a by-product . . . of having sold our souls to the entertainment industry."[12] Unrealistic expectations may create false impressions about liturgy. This is a major pitfall from which we are struggling to release ourselves. In this regard, Mark Searle writes, "The call for allowing more room to the imagination in liturgy is one that can be (and has been) misunderstood. My point is not that we need to come up with imaginative alternatives to the rites we have received (in the manner of so-called 'creative liturgies'), but that we need to recognize that the language of the rite is primarily directed to the imagination."[13] Liturgy with children, then, should lead them toward mature faith and an understanding of who they are as the baptized and an experience of how we pray the prayer of the church as members of the household of faith.

Acknowledging the restored connection of faith and worship, liturgy is a formative experience that shapes and reshapes us in our Roman Catholic identity. Therefore, children need to experience liturgy that breaks open the eternal covenant of God's never-ending love made real through the story of a baby born in a manger, the surrender on Calvary, and the triumph of the cross through the resurrection. Children do have the ability to embrace this and make it their own.

A Second Look at the *Directory for Masses with Children*[14]

The *Directory for Masses with Children* (DMC) is still relevant. Revisiting it, however, raises questions about its effectiveness, reveals its limitations, and asks challenging questions for pastoral practice with the hope of generating more meaningful possibilities for the future. Regular reference and appropriate interpretation of DMC can ensure that children are shown how to pray in a way that is effective and recognizes them as baptized members of the assembly.

In 1973, the Congregation for Divine Worship issued DMC. It is important to note that the document's inspiration was the Second Vatican Council, especially *Sacrosanctum Concilium* (Constitution on the Sacred Liturgy). Designed to serve as a supplement for the 1969 *General Instruction of the Roman Missal,* DMC's goal is to lead preadolescent children to better participation with the adult assembly. DMC also emphasizes the important connection between liturgy and Christian identity. Currently, DMC serves as a supplement to the *Third Edition of the Roman Missal.*

In general, the DMC allows for flexibility in the celebration of Masses with adults where children also participate and in Masses with children where only a few adults participate. Noteworthy is the language used in DMC. Reference to Masses *with* children, rather than Masses *for* children or *children's* Masses, is significant because only one Order of Mass exists. Rightly, liturgy gathers together all God's people.

The final paragraph of the DMC captures its essence: "The contents of the Directory have as their purpose to help children readily and joyfully encounter Christ together in the eucharistic celebration and to stand with him in the presence of the Father" (55). The DMC therefore has as its ultimate goal that children come to know Jesus Christ! Notably, this is also the goal of catechesis.[15]

The DMC holds its place as a landmark document in its efforts toward adaptation and ritual flexibility. Special concern for preadolescent children is paramount, and there is a significant shift toward the responsibility of the family. The emphasis on community and liturgical catechesis is also noteworthy.

It cannot be emphasized enough: the DMC cannot be read in isolation. Those who prepare liturgies with children need to be conversant with the fundamental principles and guidelines offered in the *Constitution on the Sacred Liturgy* and other conciliar and postconciliar documents. For example, the *General Instruction of the Roman Missal* (2011), the *Rite of Christian Initiation of Adults* (1988), the *Introduction to the Lectionary for Masses with Children* (1993), and *Sing to the Lord: Music in Divine Worship* (2007) all provide necessary background for the principles found in the DMC.

Chapter 2 of the DMC, "Masses with Adults in Which Children also Participate," seems to be the inspiration for the practice commonly known as "Family Mass." The "Family Mass" presumably came about with increased acknowledgment of the importance of the role of the family (DMC 10). DMC 16 highlights the advantage of children participating in the Mass with their family. Permission is given here to use the principles of adaptation on Sundays *at times*. It is therefore the exception, not the norm. Efforts to engage children in various ministerial roles have their place, as DMC 18 points out. Weekly celebrations of the "Family Mass" may fracture the ritual prayer of the community. In the end, the purpose of *Masses with Families* is inclusion of children and adults. Caution should be taken, however, so that in practice it does not promote child-centered liturgy, thereby excluding other members of the assembly. That being the case, a most important, however much neglected aspect of the DMC is found at no. 21: "It is always necessary to keep in mind that these eucharistic celebrations lead children toward the celebration of Mass with adults, especially the Masses at which the Christian community must come together on Sundays." Children and families can be recognized on special occasions but not at the expense of anyone else's full inclusion in the assembly.

Underpinning the DMC is the imperative for *adaptation*. Chapter 3, "Masses with Children in Which Only a Few Adults Participate," elaborates on the principle of adaptation in the context of weekday celebrations of Mass with schoolchildren (which is the primary intent of the DMC). Key to our understanding is that adaptation should be faithful to liturgical principles. Adaptation is not an attempt to *create* liturgies for children. We need only to use well the gift and grace of the Order of Mass. In addition, assigning themes for Mass is not helpful. There is one theme for every Mass, that is, paschal mystery! Accordingly, in regard to adaptation, DMC 21 states, "Thus, apart from adaptations that are necessary because of the children's age, the result should not be entirely special rites, markedly different from the Order of Mass celebrated with a congregation."

The provisions found in chapter 3 of the DMC regarding modifications in environment, music, gestures, silence, and visual elements need to be interpreted in light of the *General Instruction of the Roman Missal.* It should be evident that the preparation of liturgy with children requires consistent collaboration among liturgists and catechists. Catechists need to be helped to grasp liturgical understanding of liturgy with children. Chapter 5 of this book will explore these adaptations in more detail, especially in regard to preparing First Communion liturgies.

When considering liturgy with children, as previously stated, children are natural mystics. Developmentally, children experience a profound sense of identity in and through ritual. Young children do not acquire Christian identity from a textbook. Rather, their Christian identity is formed through ritual activity that appeals to the senses. The Paschal Triduum provides a helpful example. Despite its richness, many adults argue the Triduum is not for children. I wholeheartedly disagree! I find it disappointing that the DMC does not treat feasts and seasons of the church year. Regardless, children appreciate and readily participate in rituals such as foot washing and adoration of the cross.

I am reminded of the time when in the middle of a July barbeque my young son asked, "When do we go to church and they wash people's feet?" My son's inquiry affirms that the rituals of the church leave an impact on young children. Additionally, the Easter Vigil is rich in the stories and symbols that teach young and old who we are as a Christian people. Reflecting on this, Thomas Shepard provides powerful insight: "When I was a child, the Easter Vigil was a profound event for me. I didn't know what was going on, but I did know they were doing everything I liked. They were playing with fire. They were playing with water. They were singing things I didn't understand. He was blowing on the water! He was splashing the water on people! The air was full of smoke. It was dark and it was scary. It was everything I loved. That was the beginning of liturgy for me."[16]

Ironically, as previously noted, childlike qualities are an important aspect of adult faith. A childlike attitude is essential for full, active, and conscious participation in the life, death, and resurrection of Christ. By its very nature, liturgy presupposes a childlike faith that engages the imagination in order to experience the presence of God here and now. In the liturgy, transformation occurs if we be like little children—open to the God of surprises. In reality, everyone is a child of God. An overly strong sense of factions and cohorts should not predominate when the community gathers in faithful companionship around the Lord's Table.

Critical reflection on the DMC suggests important implications for the celebration of liturgy with children, and for our purpose here, for First Communion. Therefore, as we prepare the liturgy for First Communion, I suggest serious consideration of the following reflections:

- Have we taken adaptation too far? Does the DMC serve best as a resource for catechesis *toward* liturgy?

- Has the expectation to lead children to participation created an audience of adults with children performing all of the ministries?

- Have we unnecessarily put children on display at Mass? Has inclusion of children and their families led to exclusion of others in the assembly?

- Is there the expectation and acceptance for entertainment at Mass? Have we underestimated the natural tendency of children toward the mystical?

- And most important, have we failed to show children how to pray by focusing on the entertainment of it all?

Careful consideration of the *Directory for Masses with Children* provokes much-needed attention to the role of children in the liturgical life of the church, and, at the same time, much-needed attention to the importance of celebrating all liturgy well. It is the liturgy, after all, that forms us in our way of being in the world.

Children as Members of the Assembly

A common misconception is the reference to children as the future of the church. While this is true in some regard, baptized children ought to be acknowledged as the church *now*. In doing so, we recognize the presence of the Holy Spirit within them. Adults ought to consistently respect the dignity of children, as well as children's place in the church. This reality sheds light on how we view the role of children in the worshipping assembly. The ideal liturgical assembly, writes Mark Searle, "is a gathering of all God's people in a given place: men, women, children, the elderly, the sick, representatives of every social group and stratum. This is the church most visible as what she is: the work of Christ, gathering the scattered children of God into one."[17] This viewpoint leads us toward a deeper understanding and richer experience of our profound religious identity. This identity, particularly for children, then, develops within the worshipping assembly.

There was a time that a parish offered a well-developed preschool catechetical program for four- and five-year-old children. It was scheduled for Sunday mornings at the same time the "Family Mass" was celebrated. Of course, there was the expectation that the parents of the young children would attend Mass while their children attended religious classes. It became apparent, however, that while many were attending Mass, others were dropping their children off, filling the time with other activities such as shopping or a relaxing Sunday brunch. Needless to say, the Sunday preschool religion program was phased out gradually. Alternatively, parents were encouraged to understand that their four- and five-year-old children needed to be at Mass—*with* their parents. There is something extremely formative about families worshipping together that cannot be missed. For example, I once observed a father carefully showing his young child what page to turn to in the hymnal. Regardless of whether the child could read or sing the hymn, the child was learning what we do when we go to Mass.

Many people might remember a time when parochial schoolchildren were required to attend Sunday Mass with their class. The above reflection on DMC illustrates a shift from this practice and with good reason. Together, children and adults shape the worshipping assembly and experience God's presence among us. Significantly, this is the optimum way to prepare for the celebration of First Communion, the subject of chapter 4.

Children form an important part of the liturgical assembly; therefore, we need to provide children with liturgies that proclaim and celebrate the mystery of God in our midst. In order to allow this to happen, consistent connections must be made with the liturgical activity of the church and the everyday lives of families. Remember that religious identity is also formed in the home. The Dogmatic Constitution on the Church (*Lumen Gentium*) states, "In what might be regarded as the domestic Church, the parents, by word and example, are the first heralds of the faith with regard to their children" (LG 11). This thought-provoking metaphor merits our attention, as it makes clear that families are sacred and holy, while also acknowledging that families are not to exist in isolation. In this regard it may be helpful to recognize, for example, the importance of meals shared in the home. However, we also must be sensitive to the reality that many families are fraught with hardship and obligations every day. They often rush from one activity to the next, skipping meals entirely or providing them on the run or in front of the television. In contrast, a ritual of mealtime may be a sacred time that offers the family an opportunity to come together and listen to one another. One suggestion might be to encourage busy families to have at least one such evening meal during the week, where the whole family comes together and shares its stories. I am reminded of one particular family that made Friday night pizza a special event. In preparation for Sunday Eucharist (as prescribed by the parish catechetical program), they gathered at the kitchen table, lit a candle, said a prayer, read the Sunday readings, and spent the remainder of their meal discussing and sharing thoughts on the readings. They gave particular attention to what the readings were calling them to do. It is interesting to note that this family included four children from ages six to sixteen and two parents who both worked outside the home and took part in various community activities. Pizza night became a weekly ritual that was meaningful for the whole family.

The "domestic church" forms the eucharistic assembly. Therefore, care needs to be taken not to expose children to Mass that is entertainment-driven, that is geared to appeal to what adults think children will appreciate, that includes homilies focused solely on children (ignoring the adults present), that showcases children instead of including them, and that features music esthetically poor and theologically deficient. Children who are perpetually exposed to what is commonly referred to, although inaccurately, "Children's Mass" or "Family Mass" will not develop an appreciation for full, active, and conscious participation in its most authentic sense.

Many bishops, priests, teachers, and pastoral ministers validly express the crisis of Catholic identity today. One of the most important ways to "fix" this, in my view, is with ardent attention to how we celebrate liturgy *with* children. Practically speaking, involving children should not be to showcase them but to teach them how to minister. We don't involve children merely for the sake of involving them; children and adults can minister together where appropriate, for example, as greeters. In order for this to be accomplished proficiently, liturgical education is needed for all who teach, lead, and volunteer in both the educational and liturgical ministries of the church.

Chapters 4 and 5 of *First Communion Liturgies* explore practical suggestions for making these reflections a reality in regard to the celebration of First Communion. To better understand our current reality and how we may need to adjust our practice, let us first turn and place First Communion in its appropriate historical context, the subject of the next chapter.

2

Developing Patterns of First Communion

The eucharistic mystery is truly the center of the liturgy and indeed of the whole Christian life. Consequently the Church, guided by the Holy Spirit, continually seeks to understand this mystery more fully and more and more to derive its life from it.

—*Eucharisticum Mysterium* 1

A brief look at the developing patterns for the reception of First Communion will provide us with a greater appreciation for contemporary liturgical practice. As we will see, the Second Vatican Council recovered the meaning of the Eucharist as a sacrament of initiation. This has been made especially clear with the restoration of the *Rite of Christian Initiation of Adults* (RCIA) in 1972; however, there was a time when the Western church did not regard Eucharist as an initiation sacrament. Prior to Vatican II there was little to suggest the intimate connection of the reception of Holy Communion with baptism. History reveals that this disconnection was not always the case.[1]

18

Early Ritual and Practice

Early church documents, for example, the *Didache*, *Didascalia*, and the *Apostolic Tradition*, reveal that regardless of a person's age, Eucharist was part of the baptismal rites of the church. The *Apology of Justin Martyr* and Cyprian of Carthage also noted that the Eucharist belonged to the baptized. Therefore, it is quite evident that early church ritual and practice affirm that infants and children received Communion at the time of their baptism. Since participation in the Eucharist was reserved for the baptized, there was great significance in "the baptismal Eucharist."[2] In other words, there was a profound relationship between baptism and Eucharist.

During the "Golden Age" (301–500) when Christianity was declared the official religion of the Roman Empire, the rites of initiation became even more profound. Those initiated into the church, regardless of age, celebrated baptism, what we now know as confirmation, and Communion during the Easter Vigil. Paul Turner poetically describes the mood of such ritual: "Characterized by ample ritual gestures and beautifully crafted prayers, the initiation rites entered a golden age, presenting the drama of the paschal mystery alive within the community of believers."[3] Similarly, Egeria, a fourth-century Spanish nun visiting Jerusalem during Holy Week, most likely in the presence of bishop Cyril (c.315–c.387),[4] reports in her journal, "While the congregation . . . kept the paschal vigil in the Martyrium, the candidates went into the baptistery and were baptized. Then they were clothed in white and went with the bishop to the Anastasis, where there was a psalm and a prayer said for them. After that, they went to join the congregation of the faithful in the Martyrium and received Holy Communion for the first time."[5]

Those who are familiar with the RCIA know this early history well because it impacted the restoration of the

catechumenate. Moreover, much liturgical and ecclesial richness was born out of the *Rite of Christian Initiation of Adults*,
approved by Pope Paul VI in 1972 and mandated for use in
the United States in 1988. Keep in mind that throughout
this book, we will notice the strong impact of the RCIA
upon both catechesis and liturgies for First Communion.

New Practices

As the church grew in numbers, initiation practices began
to change. Although the sequence of baptism, confirmation, and Eucharist remained intact for the most part, over
time they were no longer celebrated at the same ritual.
Due to the fact that confirmation was associated with the
bishop, it was necessary to delay it until the bishop could
be present, however, in such cases baptismal Communion
was still given; thus we begin to see a disruption in the
order for the initiation rituals. From the sixth through ninth
centuries, different patterns begin to emerge. As we know,
in the East the sequence of rites remained unified; in the
West, however, different sequences coexisted, depending
on whether the bishop presided or not. To this day, with
the implementation of the catechumenate with children,
different sequences continue to coexist with good reason.

Due to the varied practices of the initiation rites, during
the period between the late tenth century and the thir-
teenth century, we continue to see the appearance of erratic
practices. In many cases, the long tradition of infant and
children's Communion at baptism began to be disregarded.
In time, due to the infrequent reception of Communion in
general, partly because of feelings of unworthiness among
the faithful, it seemed unnecessary to give Communion to
the newly baptized.

By the early sixteenth century, baptismal Eucharist fell out
of practice, thus weakening the connection of Communion

with baptism. Reference to the full initiation of infants gradually vanished. Moreover, great devotion and reverence for the Eucharist grew, feelings of unworthiness to receive Communion increased, and proper understanding of the sacrament before receiving it was considered to be necessary.

It is important to note that the Fourth Lateran Council (1215), three hundred years before, did not forbid infant Communion; it influenced, however, the future practice because it "marked the beginning of a new practice in the Latin Church."[6] In this regard, Turner writes:

> The Fourth Lateran Council (1215) served as a watershed for the history of the age of the candidate and the sequence of the sacraments of baptism, confirmation, and Eucharist. It decreed that every Christian should confess his or her sins once a year after reaching the "years of discretion." It also asked people to fulfill their penance and receive Communion during the season of Easter. The council did not require the deferral of Communion to the age of discretion or confession before every Communion, but it set up a rhythm that allowed those applications. Also, by requesting that the Christian receive Communion "reverently," Lateran IV laid the groundwork for making devotion part of a child's preparation for the first reception of Communion.[7]

In addition, Aquinas confirmed that children needed to demonstrate use of reason and devotion to the sacrament (ST III, q. 80, a. 9, ad. 3). In view of these developments, it became common practice for catechesis to precede the first reception of Holy Communion. There was the expectation that before the reception of First Communion some form of intellectual and moral capacity would be demonstrated. Therefore, First Communion gradually took place at about the age of ten or twelve. It is interesting to note that there is no evidence of a formal ceremony for First Communion during this time.

The Council of Trent

Twenty-eight years after Martin Luther posted his Ninety-Five Theses, the Council of Trent (1545–1563) convened. It was a long, complex event that had theological, ecclesial, and political ramifications.[8] During an eighteen-year span, three popes convened the council amidst countless interruptions and obstacles. The Council of Trent articulated the meaning of Catholicism in a world where Catholic was no longer the only Christian religion in Europe.[9] The council's decrees touched practically every aspect of Catholic life, giving rise to a deeper sense of identity for the Catholic Christian.

Sacraments and the doctrine of the Eucharist were among some of the most important topics of the council's weighty agenda. Regarding the celebration of First Communion, Trent affirmed Lateran IV, and decreed "that it is not required that children receive communion before they 'reach the age of discernment'" (726–728).[10] Opinion varied, however, as to what age this actually was, and some made a distinction for the age for confessing sin and the age for receiving Communion. Following this decree, children were to receive their First Communion at about ten to fourteen years of age, which remained the case until the early twentieth century.

Pius X: Pope of the Eucharist

As we have learned, there have been variations regarding age and disposition for the celebration for First Communion since the beginnings of our church. On August 8, 1910, the Sacred Congregation of the Sacraments, with the approval of Pope Pius X, issued the Decree on the Age of Children Who Are to be Admitted to First Holy Communion (*Quam Singulari*), which is considered the most important legislation dealing with the First Communion of children since the Council of Trent. As we will see, this document presents a clear regulation for admission to the Eucharist. But first, we should explore the impetus behind this particular directive.

From the beginning of his life as a priest, Pius X had a sincere concern for the church, especially in regard to catechesis and preparing children for sacraments. In fact, due to his passion for teaching children, Pius X became known as the "Pope of the Little Children."[11] Overall, it disturbed Pius X that God seemed absent from the ordinary lives of people. He feared that grave problems troubled human society, and religious regeneration was in order. For this reason, his first encyclical letter, The Restoration of All Things in Christ (*E Supremi Apostolatus*), issued on October 4, 1903, aimed to bring "human society, now estranged from the wisdom of Christ, back to the discipline of the Church."[12]

Pius X believed deeply that education in faith would revitalize the church. To further his cause, during his pontificate, Pius X issued over thirty catechetical documents.[13] He advocated for good catechetical instruction for both young and old. Moreover, he believed that, in addition to the clergy, trained laypeople were also responsible for teaching.

Against the backdrop of both modern thought and Jansenism (a religious movement that stressed human unworthiness), which was still influencing Catholicism, Pius X is particularly noted for his decrees on Holy Communion. It is for this reason that Pius X is often referred to as the Pope of the Eucharist. Prior to the above-mentioned *Quam Singulari* in 1910, the Decree on the Necessary Disposition for Frequent and Daily Reception of Holy Communion (*Sacra Tridentina Synodus*) was issued on December 20, 1905. This document, a prelude to the very significant *Quam Singulari,* echoes the Council of Trent, which supported frequent reception of Communion.[14] For well over a thousand years, lay Catholics received Communion, at most, once a year on Easter or Pentecost. Regarding the accomplishment of Pius X, Robert Taft writes, "The greatest and most successful liturgical reform in Catholic history is surely the movement for the restoration of frequent communion, sanctioned by Pius X in 1906. There are still pockets of resistance, and there are abuses, but nothing can detract from this great pastoral victory that has turned around fifteen centuries of devotional history in fifty years."[15] Besides appreciating the early history of the church, this pastoral change positively aided in making the Mass an important event in the life of the Roman Catholic, ended the lay/clergy distinction, and gave people a sense of worthiness. Significantly, as noted by Joseph Dougherty, *Sacra Tridentina Synodus* "reveals a shift in attitude toward the sacraments and toward the relationship between the world and the transcendent."[16]

Quam Singulari (QS) was very effective in its clarity of vision. The document reflects on Christ's love for children, the ancient practice of the baptismal Communion, the legislation at the Fourth Lateran Council, the Council of Trent, the teaching of St. Thomas Aquinas, and Pope Pius IX, who disapproved of delaying First Communion. Most important, QS settled a centuries-old dilemma regarding the age of First Communion and the knowledge necessary prior to receiving Communion. In this regard, three significant passages from QS are:

> The age of discretion, both for Confession and for Holy Communion, is the time when a child begins to reason, that is about the seventh year, more or less. From that time on begins the obligation of fulfilling the precept of both Confession and Communion. (QS I)[17]

> A full and perfect knowledge of Christian doctrine is not necessary either for First Confession or for First Communion. Afterwards, however, the child will be obliged to learn gradually the entire Catechism according to his ability. (QS 2)

> The knowledge of religion which is required in a child in order to be properly prepared to receive First Communion

is such that he will understand according to his capacity those Mysteries of faith which are necessary as a means of salvation . . . and that he can distinguish between the Bread of the Eucharist and ordinary, material bread, and thus he may receive Holy Communion with a devotion becoming his years. (QS 3)

QS further states, "The obligation of the precept of Confession and Communion which binds the child particularly affects those who have him in charge, namely, parents, confessors, teachers, and pastors (QS 4). The document continues, "The pastor should announce and hold a General Communion of the children at least once a year or more often, and he should on those occasions admit not only the First Communicants but also others who have already approached the Holy Table with the above-mentioned consent of their parents or confessor" (QS 5).

The work of Pius X most likely seemed new for its time. We can see, however, how it builds on ancient practice, the Council of Trent, and the work of St. Thomas Aquinas. And we can be certain that this change was not made overnight. In fact, over twenty years ago I remember hearing students reflect on the experiences of their grandparents who received First Communion at a later age, long after 1910. Moreover, as noted by Paul Marx, OSB, in his work, *Virgil Michel and the Liturgical Movement*:

In 1910 Catholics the world over raised eyebrows when the holy pontiff lowered the age for reception of first Communion from the usual twelve or thirteen to the age when reason dawns. How long was it before pastors in the United States accepted the papal directive? It would be difficult to say exactly, but from all indications there was much neglect. For instance, Father Fidelis Busam, O.S.B., of St. Vincent Archabbey, complained in a letter to Michel on December 14, 1926, that 'there are not many pastors who observe the

> decree of Pius X on frequent and daily communion.' Another
> pastor stated as late as 1929: "I almost had to defend myself
> with a gun because I introduced the custom of taking the
> little ones to first Communion at the age set down in the
> decree of Pius X. I was besieged on all sides with arguments
> about the incapability of these little ones to understand
> what it was all about, not to say anything about their being
> capable of learning sufficient catechism."[18]

Our experiences of contemporary disagreements, for example, regarding the revised English Translation of the
Roman Missal in 2011, demonstrate that people are no
different today than they were in the time of Pius X.

Consideration of the history of First Communion brings
to our realization that Pius X is but one piece of the liturgical and catechetical puzzle of our church. He certainly
displayed sound pastoral practice and astute decisiveness.
The movement for frequent Communion, and in turn, low-
ering the age for the reception of First Communion, brought
Catholic children and adults toward a "new sacramental
praxis."[19] More work was needed, however; for example,
Keith Pecklers notes that Lambert Beauduin, a key figure of
the liturgical movement in Belgium, "was bothered by the
fact that Pius X's decree on frequent Communion in 1905
failed to stress the reality that Communion was an integral
part of the Mass itself."[20] We can concur, however, that the
concerns of Pius X set the stage for the continuing efforts
toward liturgical reform.

The Liturgical Movement

Significant to our reflection is the often forgotten liturgical movement of the early twentieth century. There is no
doubt that the ongoing liturgical agenda of the Catholic
Church has a direct influence on the celebration of First
Communion today. Having its roots in Europe, the early

liturgical movement paved the way and laid the ground-work for the reform of the liturgy initiated with the Second Vatican Council. The gradual changes that were eventually set in motion through Vatican II can be found in the work of liturgical scholars, both clergy and lay.

Foremost among the early liturgical pioneers is Virgil Michel, OSB (1890–1938), often accepted as the founder of the liturgical movement in the United States. Michel's work echoes that of Pius X and Pius XI, who called for a renewal of the Christian spirit, which Michel believed was renewed through the liturgy. In turn, the basic ideal of the liturgy can be found in the doctrine of the Mystical Body of Christ, a key theme of his writing.[21] Often to the detriment of his health, Michel labored passionately to create the awareness that liturgy could be more effective in people's lives. To this end, he ardently believed, much like Pius X, that education was key to understanding the theological foundation of the liturgy. In order to make his vision a reality, Michel founded the Liturgical Press and *Orate Fratres* (now *Worship*) in 1926. He used these vehicles for ideas to teach about Eucharist and its implications for a way of being in the world. His writings are as relevant now as they were during his life-time. In addition, publications from the above-mentioned sources continue to inspire and educate people throughout the world about important liturgical matters.

Equally concerned for liturgical matters, Pius XII led the Catholic Church during some of the most difficult times in world history. He believed that the world could heal the wounds of war, for example, through meaningful ritual prayer. In this regard, he recognized the work of Virgil Michel and his brother Benedictines. And his encyclical *Mediator Dei* (1947) states: "You are of course familiar with the fact, Venerable Brethren, that a remarkably widespread revival of scholarly interest in the sacred liturgy took place toward the end of the last century and has continued through the early years of this one. The movement owed its rise to commendable private initiative and more particularly to the zealous and persistent labor of several monasteries within the distinguished Order of Saint Benedict" (MD 4). It is no surprise, then, that Pius XII's encyclicals, notably On the Mystical Body of Christ (*Mystici Corporis Christi*) in 1943, and especially On the Sacred Liturgy (*Mediator Dei*) in 1947, were, as Keith Pecklers writes, " the culmination of years of liturgical pioneering."[22] In addition to the work of the early liturgical movement, both of these documents greatly influenced liturgical theology that, as we will explore in subsequent chapters, has implications for the celebration of First Holy Communion.

The liturgical movement planted the seeds for the Second Vatican Council, particularly in regard to the principle of active participation. Active participation was the "point of departure" for integrating liturgy, education, and social justice.[23] It is this call to participation that was a major component of the liturgical renewal of Vatican II, and as we are aware, regarding the celebration of the Eucharist, has meaning beyond the obvious.

The Second Vatican Council

The Second Vatican Council is the part of the developing patterns with which we are most familiar. Although the council does not deal with the issue of First Communion explicitly, it does, however, address a renewed theology of sacraments that directly affects how we celebrate a child's First Communion. One notable document, the Constitution on the Sacred Liturgy (*Sacrosanctum Concilium*), promulgated on December 4, 1963, states: "The sacred Council has set out to impart an ever-increasing vigor to the Christian life of the faithful; to adapt more closely to the needs of our age those institutions which are subject to change; to foster whatever can promote union among all who believe in Christ; to strengthen whatever can help to call all mankind into the Church's fold. Accordingly it sees particularly cogent reasons for undertaking the reform and promotion of the liturgy" (SC 1).[24] The document goes on to say that it is through the Eucharist that the faithful express the mystery of Christ (SC 2). It is interesting to note that one can glean a sense of continuity with the message of Pius X.

With the above statements from *Sacrosanctum Concilium* as the introduction to the rest of the document, this historic statement of the church, pronounced fifty years ago, goes on to scrutinize sacraments, particularly baptism, confirmation, and Eucharist. It called for a revision of the rite of baptism for infants (SC 67), emphasizing the role of parents and godparents. Significantly, the document called for a restoration of the catechumenate for adults (SC 64), which as previously mentioned has deep implications for our understanding of the sacraments of initiation. As we will discover, this restoration impacts not only our understanding of Eucharist as initiation but the manner in which we understand and implement the craft of catechesis. Additionally, the rite of Confirmation was to be revised to make the connection with Christian initiation apparent (SC 71). Outstandingly, regarding the Eucharist, the document states:

> The Church, therefore, earnestly desires that Christ's faithful, when present at this mystery of faith, should not be there as strangers or silent spectators. On the contrary, through a good understanding of the rites and prayers, they should take part in the sacred action, conscious of what they are doing, with devotion and full collaboration. They should be instructed by God's word, and be nourished at the table of the Lord's Body. They should give thanks to God. Offering the immaculate victim, not only through the hands of the priest but also together with him, they should learn to offer themselves. (SC 48)

This cannot be taken lightly, for it has profound implications with regard to how we celebrate First Communion.

The recovery of a sense of initiation is made more clearly in Dogmatic Constitution on the Church (*Lumen Gentium*). In other words, the rediscovery of the nature of church as the People of God fosters a community structure, which is made known to us through the sacraments of baptism, confirmation, and Eucharist. In this regard, *Lumen Gentium* states:

> Incorporated into the Church by Baptism, the faithful are appointed by their baptismal character to Christian religious worship; reborn as sons of God, they must profess before men the faith they have received from God through the Church. By the sacrament of Confirmation they are more perfectly bound to the Church and are endowed with the special strength of the Holy Spirit. Hence, they are, true witnesses of Christ, more strictly obliged to spread the faith by word and deed.
>
> Taking part in the Eucharistic sacrifice, the source and summit of the Christian life, they offer the divine victim to God and themselves along with it. And so it is that, both in the offering and in Holy Communion, each in his own way, though not of course indiscriminately, has his own part to play in the liturgical action. Then, strengthened by the body of Christ in the eucharistic communion, they manifest in a concrete way that unity of the People of God which this holy sacrament aptly signifies and admirably realizes. (LG 11)

In and through the reforms of the twentieth century, the church reclaims the notion of a community gathered as one Body, united in the memory of Jesus Christ. Baptism, confirmation, and particularly Eucharist express this common bond. In turn, Vatican II recovered the role of the liturgical assembly, called into being through the grace-filled initiative of God. Through the celebration of the Eucharist, God speaks and we respond.

First Communion Rituals:
A Grassroots Movement

As previously noted, from early on there was no ritual specific to First Communion. In the early church, remember, the child's first reception of Communion was part of the baptism ritual. When baptismal Eucharist fell out of practice there was often a substitute, for example, bringing the child to the altar or giving him or her unconsecrated wine.[25] After the Council of Trent when an educational process for First Communion began to take root, catechesis prior to First Communion served to instill a sense of devotion to the Eucharist in the child. In addition, since confession was expected prior to First Communion we can presume that moral behavior was also part of catechesis for First Communion. Emphasis clearly shifted away from thoughts of initiation toward intellectual development and moral maturity.

Although Rome supported but never endorsed a ritual for First Communion, the appearance of formal rituals celebrated with groups of children began in the Roman Catholic Church in France in about the year 1593. These rituals gained popularity and spread throughout the Catholic world within the next fifty years.[26] Prior to this time, it is interesting to note that a public ceremony for First Communion with children developed in the Protestant Church.[27] The French ritual, celebrated with groups of children, most likely developed as a result of educating children in faith together. Dioceses and religious communities in particular regulated the ceremonies, which incidentally were never authorized by Rome.

Peter McGrail writes, "The development of a special 'Mass of First Communion' at which all the children of a given age-determined cohort were admitted to the eucharist together, considerably raised the public profile of the event. This was no longer simply an intensely personal and essentially private moment, linked to an individual child's human development; instead it could become a highly visible spectacle of faith and devotion for the parish community as a whole."[28]

There is also some evidence that these rituals extended beyond Mass. For example, Vespers, processions, renewal of baptismal promises, and consecration to the Blessed Mother took place on the following day.[29] The custom of white clothes began with the Ursuline sisters and can be interpreted as reminiscent of the baptismal garment. Others thought that the white attire was in imitation of angels.

Roman Catholic rituals for First Communion were part of a grassroots movement and were passed down through the years by personal testimony.[30] Devotional in nature, the First Communion ritual was meant to inspire children and instill in them a sense of remembrance. The adult community generally watched as children received communion, which appealed to people on the emotional level. Moreover, the reception of Communion was still uncommon for adult Catholics; therefore, these rituals stirred the desire to receive Communion for those who witnessed the ceremony.

As we have seen, much has developed through the centuries; however, regarding the rituals for First Communion, in some cases, very little has changed. People often resist pastoral efforts to revise the ceremony to be more in keeping with the theology of the sacrament. First Communion liturgies should echo the deep meaning of what it means to be a member of the Body of Christ.

First Communion in the United States

In relation to pertinent segments of history discussed previously, a look at the celebration of First Communion in the United States may be beneficial.

In the years following the Council of Trent, many synods and councils were held throughout Europe and the United

States. At the I Synod of Baltimore (1791) Bishop Carroll "decreed that pastors should not unduly defer the first Holy Communion of children, nor allow them to receive It immediately after attaining the use of reason."[31] At II Plenary Council of Baltimore (1866) pastors were charged with judging the child's readiness to receive. In addition, the council at Baltimore valued the opinion of St. Thomas Aquinas in regard to the use of reason and declared the age for celebrating First Communion ten to fourteen.[32]

The official establishment of a later age for First Communion mandated that a child attend catechism classes for at least two years. Children needed to know the difference between ordinary bread and the Body and Blood of Jesus. In addition, they needed to learn how to approach the sacrament with dignity and reverence. This attitude survived well into the years leading up to Vatican II. After Vatican II, changes occurred that led to a different tone, especially in regard to First Communion liturgies. Jo-Ann Metzdorff maintains that consumerism affects attitudes toward faith, in particular how families approach the celebration of First Communion.[33]

This brief look at the developing patterns for the celebration and preparation for First Communion provides for us some important background as the contemporary story unfolds. By examining the theology of the Eucharist in the next chapter, we might gain a deeper sense of how we can better prepare and celebrate a child's First Communion.

3

First Communion in Context

When a community is a Christian community, one of the central patterns and rhythms it develops is a communal life of prayer, a characteristic set of forms for addressing the mystery of God.

—Maria Harris[1]

As previously noted, children have a natural sense of wonder and awe. As experts at imaginative play, children possess perceptible qualities that deem them open, dependent, and vulnerable. The openness, dependence, and vulnerability are the qualities that bring us all closer to the divine. I was once acquainted with an eight-year-old child with multiple special needs. Despite his needs and serious health issues, Matthew (not his real name) took part in the parish catechetical program on a limited basis because his parents expressed a strong desire for him to receive First Holy Communion.

In the weeks before First Communion Day, Matthew's mother became very anxious due to the fact that he was cautious about accepting anything from someone he did not know. Therefore, there was the worry that he would not take Communion from the priest.

Due to his special needs Matthew also had the assistance of an aide in school. He was very comfortable with the aide, who incidentally happened to be an Extraordinary Minister of Holy Communion. Brilliant! The parish arranged to have the aide present on First Communion Day. On the day of final preparation, the family's anxiety grew. When the parish representative reviewed the Communion procession with the children, Matthew would not take the unconsecrated host from anyone, not even his aide. Sadly, the family contemplated not having him receive Communion the following day.

There was something special about this child, so the parish advised that the parents come, and wait and see. A true spirit of love was evident. The parish community knew Matthew and rejoiced in the fact that he was participating in the celebration of First Communion. On First Communion Day, when it was time for the Communion procession, his aide was stationed as an Extraordinary Minister of Holy Communion in close proximity to the priest (Father was informed ahead of time about the situation). Matthew reverently processed, with his family, toward the altar. As the aide was ready to utter the words, "the Body of Christ," Matthew shook his head no, pointed to the priest, and formed his hands appropriately to receive Communion. Needless to say, he was the great teacher for the community on that day. Sharing this story not only demonstrates the innate connection of children with the sacred, it uncovers the investment of a community in the life of this child who was coming to the eucharistic table for the first time.

Although many children with special needs attend parish catechetical programs, many parents of these children actually question whether their children will be able to receive First Communion. This may be due to the fact that

Code of Canon Law states, "The administration of the Most Holy Eucharist to children requires that they have sufficient knowledge and careful preparation so that they understand the mystery of Christ according to their capacity and are able to receive the body of Christ with faith and devotion" (CCL 913). However, a commentary on this canon maintains, "The careful preparation required is something more than the intellectual preparation indicated by the words 'sufficient knowledge.' It includes formative experiences in faith such as promoted by active participation in the Eucharist even before the children receive the first holy communion."[2]

This commentary sheds much-needed light on why persons with developmental disabilities may receive Holy Communion. In addition, regarding children with special needs, Davis Rizzo writes, "They mediate senses such as touch, hearing, and bodily awareness. They are more imagistic and associational. This sort of sensory, visual, and experiential processing matches the spiritual understanding that comes from participation in the sacraments. The sacraments are one of the best ways to engage such children in religious and spiritual learning. They *need* the sacraments."[3] Furthermore, *Guidelines for the Celebration of the Sacraments with Persons with Disabilities* (GCSPD) affirm the criterion for receiving Communion; however, it notes that a person with developmental or mental disabilities may illustrate readiness through gesture or silence rather than verbally (GCSPD 20).

Undeniably, a child's First Communion is a moment of profound joy for children and their families, and yet the context of a child's First Communion is the communal celebration of the Eucharist. Although the role of the family never loses its significance for formation in faith (chapter 4), the parish celebration of the Eucharist teaches children, week after week, what it means to be a baptized member of the church; what it means to be in communion with one another; what it means to be one with Christ. The parish community is a community rooted in love, it is the reality of Christian life, and this reality is expressed in and through the celebration of the Eucharist. Full appreciation for the celebration of First Communion, therefore, involves viewing it in the context of the wider understanding of the church and its liturgical practices, particularly the Eucharist.

This chapter in no way exhausts the profound mystery of the Eucharist; it explores, however, some of the significant theological and liturgical perspectives helpful for an understanding of the celebration of First Communion within the wider context of the church. In doing so we can better recognize its genuine meaning and deep significance for the life of the Catholic Christian community. Significantly, in this chapter, and throughout the book, the reader will realize that the restoration of the *Rite of Christian Initiation of Adults* (RCIA) influences this contextual understanding in a very profound way.

In order to highlight the church's celebration of the Eucharist as the context for First Communion, this chapter offers a liturgical theology for the Eucharist. This theology is explored in six sections: *Eucharist, Center of Christian Life*; *Eucharist, Gathering the Body of Christ*; *Eucharist, Sacrament of Initiation*; *Eucharist, Participation in Paschal Mystery*; *Eucharist, Washing Feet*; *Eucharist, Memory and Imagination*.

Eucharist, Center of Christian Life

Throughout this book, when I refer to the Eucharist, I mean the celebration of Eucharist, the Mass. Confusion sometimes occurs because we also use the term Eucharist to refer to Holy Communion. While this is not inappropriate, for our purpose clarity is essential. In addition, I maintain that words matter, and how we use words speaks to the depth of meaning entwined within the words. It is for this reason that you will notice that throughout this book I refer to *First Communion* and not *First Eucharist* (it is the hope that it is not the child's First Eucharist). In other words, as we will see, the celebration of the Eucharist is the context for First Communion.

Most important, the celebration of the Eucharist shapes the meaning of Communion. In *Models of the Eucharist*, Kevin Irwin enumerates on several models of Eucharist that give insight into the theological and pastoral meaning of this sacrament. Irwin writes, "At issue is the theological meaning of what we say and do—what is spoken and enacted—in the liturgy. Theological shorthand often calls this the *lex orandi*, the 'law of prayer,' which influences the *lex credendi*, 'the law of belief,' meaning what the church believes."[4] For, as we know, the heart and center of Catholic life is the Eucharist. And, as such, the Eucharist has a dynamic character. It is what takes place when we gather as the baptized, hear the word of God proclaimed, profess our faith, pray for the needs of the church and the world, offer thanks and praise, come to the table, and are called to go forth in mission. The Eucharist is where we meet Christ in a unique way, and experience his saving work now. To appreciate this dynamic reality Vatican II aptly states:

> To accomplish so great a work Christ is always present in his Church, especially in her liturgical celebrations. He is present in the Sacrifice of the Mass not only in the person of his minister, "the same now offering, through the ministry of priests, who formally offered himself on the cross," but especially in the eucharistic species. By his power he is present in the sacraments so that when anybody baptizes it is really Christ himself who baptizes. He is present in his word since it is he himself who speaks when the holy scriptures are read in the Church. Lastly, he is present when the Church prays and sings, for he has promised "where two or three are gathered together in my name there I am in the midst of them" (Mt 18:20). (SC 7)

This great work is God's self-communication with us. It is about God's activity in the world. Likewise, in and through the celebration of the Eucharist God speaks and we respond. Therefore, God's initiative makes the prayer of the people possible and forms us into an assembly of believers eager to hear stories told and ultimately respond through the reception of Holy Communion, fully aware that the purpose of all of this is to go out and be Christ in the world.

Eucharist, Gathering the Body of Christ

As we saw in the previous chapter, the developing patterns for celebrating First Communion were influenced, in part, by the theology of the time. In his work, *The Sacrament of the Eucharist,* John Laurance significantly points out, "The theology of the seven sacraments prevalent in the Catholic Church through most of the second millennium interpreted those rites more as sacred objects to be *passively* received than as *active* participations in Christ's paschal mystery. And their meaning was to be derived, not from the shape of their liturgical celebration, but from the church's official teaching, teaching typically occasioned by historical challenges to her faith. Whereas in patristic times Church writers expounded the theology of the sacraments from the rites themselves."[5]

In the early church, the Greek meaning of the Eucharist was to give thanks. The Eucharist was understood as a ritual action of the gathered assembly, the church. It is from this understanding that we recognize the church as a living community that gathers to express and proclaim the presence of God in Jesus Christ. In other words, Eucharist includes, but is broader than, the bread and wine that is offered to become the Body and Blood of Christ.

Liturgical and ecclesiological changes in the liturgy set in motion by the Second Vatican Council, most notably the recovery of an understanding of sacraments as actions of God and of the church, in addition to a recovery of the communal nature of the church, contribute to a renewed understanding of Eucharist. Both of these insights not only give dignity to the vocation of the baptized but also affirm the transformative potential of active participation in the liturgy. The mystery of the Eucharist subsequently affirms the creative positive traits of contemporary living, provides hope, and most important, *is* God's active, loving presence among us.

The weekly gathering of the Body of Christ in prayer is a profound symbol of relationships rooted in the sacraments of initiation. The gathering of the baptized for Eucharist illustrates the meaning of faith. Significantly, the *Catechism of the Catholic Church* states: "Faith is a personal act—the free response of the human person to the initiative of God who reveals himself. But faith is not an isolated act. No one can believe alone, just as no one can live alone. You have not given yourself faith and you have not given yourself life. The believer has received faith from others and should hand it on to others" (CCC 166). Within this understanding, the Eucharist, celebrated through the feasts and seasons of the liturgical year, unlocks the sacramental imagination and offers for us a particular way of being in the world. The Eucharist, therefore, imaginatively nurtures, shapes, and forms us, while at the same time instinctively provides meaning for life lived in and through the Christian community.

Eucharist, Sacrament of Initiation— Becoming the Body of Christ

From generation to generation the memory of the death and resurrection of Jesus Christ has encouraged gathering, prayer, table companionship, service, and ultimately mission. The Eucharist, the ritual action of the community of believers gathered with the risen Lord, essentially supports us in remembering who we are as the baptized. There is no doubt that greater appreciation for the celebration of the Eucharist, along with its deep meaning for the life of the baptized, requires revitalization in our time. Moreover, the 1983 Code of Canon Law (CCL) states, "The sacraments of baptism, confirmation, and the Most Holy Eucharist are interrelated in such a way that they are required for full Christian initiation" (CCL 842 §2).

The restoration of the Catechumenate, with sacramental initiation celebrated at the Easter Vigil, has accentuated the prominence of baptism, and at the same time affirms its relationship with confirmation and Eucharist. The RCIA states, "The third step in the Christian initiation of adults is the celebration of the sacraments of baptism, confirmation, and eucharist. Through this final step the elect, receiving pardon for their sins, are admitted into the people of God. They are graced with adoption as children of God and are led by the Holy Spirit into the promised fullness of time begun in Christ and, as they share in the eucharistic sacrifice and meal, even to a foretaste of the kingdom of God" (RCIA 206). Of great significance here is the restoration of the sequence and unity of the sacraments of initiation. In the context of the RCIA it is unmistakable that Eucharist is the high point of initiation. During the Easter Vigil, for example, the RCIA suggests, "Before saying 'This is the Lamb of God,' the celebrant may briefly remind the neophytes of the preeminence of the eucharist, which is the climax of their initiation and the center of the whole Christian life" (RCIA 243). In this regard, Julia Upton, in *A Church for the Next Generation: Sacraments in Transition*, writes that the RCIA "is dramatically changing the shape of the Church."[6] Currently, we are living this reality because, outside of the RCIA, it is becoming more and more apparent that baptism, confirmation, and Eucharist retain their initiatory character even when years separate their celebration. In other words, confirmation celebrated during young adulthood or adolescence is still the public affirmation of baptism, and Eucharist celebrated prior to confirmation is still the summit of Christian initiation.

The threshold for all sacraments is baptism; confirmation is best understood only when viewed in the context of baptism; and Eucharist, the only repeatable sacrament of initiation, identifies and recalls what happened at the baptismal font. In reference to the retrieval of a more traditional view for initiation spelled out in the RCIA, Aidan Kavanagh prophetically writes, "The *Rite's* norm of baptism thus rests on the economic principle that baptism is inadequately perceptible apart from the eucharist; that the eucharist is not wholly knowable without reference to conversion in faith; that conversion is abortive if it does not issue in sacramental illumination by incorporation into the Church; . . . In baptism the eucharist begins, and in the eucharist baptism is sustained."[7]

Clearly, the RCIA provides a profound impact on our understanding of the Eucharist because the journey that begins at the font is renewed with every celebration of the Eucharist. Moreover, it gives birth to a new sense of mutuality, care, and compassion for the church, our neighbor, and the world. Likewise, as Nathan Mitchell points out, "Christian ritual, prayer, and sacrament occur at the confluence of three distinct—yet essentially interdependent—liturgies: the 'liturgy of the world,' the 'liturgy of the church,' and the 'liturgy of the neighbor.'"[8] Participation in the Eucharist, then, involves a process of becoming, and presumes the conviction that the participant has accepted life in Christ, for the Eucharist is participation in the mystery of Christ's death and resurrection, while at the same time it assists and encourages a gospel-centered life.

The Christian vocation inevitably flows from an identity inherent in baptism, confirmation, and Eucharist. Therefore, participation in the Eucharist strengthens what happed at baptism and enables us to put on Christ—again. In turn, authentic participation in the Eucharist enhances our relationships and forms us in our baptismal vocation. It is for this reason when we enter the worship space that we make the sign of the cross with holy water.

Eucharist, Participation in Paschal Mystery

As Christians we are initiated for what Mark Searle refers to as the "art of participation into the liturgical prayer of the church."[9] This is a profound statement that gradually unfolds in meaning throughout a person's life. There are different levels of participation implied in the celebration of the Eucharist; most obvious is participation as engagement in the ritual prayers, hymns, gestures, Word, and sacrament. On a deeper level participation involves mystagogical reflection on our identity as members of the Body of Christ. Although in our time we are familiar with the term *mystagogy* in the context of the RCIA, *mystagogy* has deeper implications for our understanding. A broader sense of *mystagogy*, however, goes beyond the reflection of the liturgical rites.[10] *Mystagogy* is about living a mystery. It is a particular mode of existence that helps us to embrace the paschal mystery in our everyday living and dying.

The relationship of liturgy with ecclesiology is also an important consideration. A distinct eucharistic ecclesiology underlies the documents of Vatican II and provides us with deep theological implications and ecclesial sensitivity for the celebration of the Eucharist.[11] A lucid understanding of our ecclesial identity impacts yet a deeper level of participation. And Paul's Letter to the Romans makes this abundantly clear. The distinct meaning of baptism is found in this passage: "Are you unaware that we who were baptized into Christ Jesus were baptized into his death? We were indeed buried with him through baptism into death, so that, just as Christ was raised from the dead by the glory of the Father, we too might live in newness of life" (Rom 6:3-4). This reading is the linchpin of the Easter Vigil because it explicitly recalls what it means to be a member of the church. Participation in the church's eucharistic celebration, then, is participation in the life of faith which is spelled out through baptism.

Participation in the Eucharist is participation in the mystery of God experienced in and through the life, death, and resurrection of Jesus the Christ. The life of Christian faith is the mystery of Christ dead and risen. In baptism we enter Christ's tomb and rise to the fullness of new life. Therefore, active participation in the Eucharist can be nothing less than participation in paschal mystery—the mystery of Easter. Joseph Cardinal Ratzinger, now Pope Emeritus Benedict XVI, reminds us, "The Last Supper alone is not sufficient for the institution of the Eucharist. For the words that Jesus spoke then are an anticipation of his death, a transformation of his death into an event of love, a transformation of what is meaningless into something that is significant, significant for us."[12] Subsequently, active participation means to live this mystery daily, and in turn we gain insight to a life filled with awe-inspiring hope.

Paschal mystery gives living and dying new meaning. It provides patterns of hope learned in and through the story of Jesus and his disciples. In and through the celebration of the Eucharist the church calls all of us to enduring hope. In and through the celebration of the Eucharist we bring our personal story and connect it with the mystery of Christ.

Eucharist, Washing Feet

The church provides us with the profound meaning of Eucharist on Holy Thursday night when we gather for the first movement of the Paschal Triduum, the Mass of the Lord's Supper. The Mass of the Lord's Supper demonstrates the depth of the Christian story. It shows us who we are, and who we are meant to be, namely, a people called to service. The reading from Paul's First Letter to the Corinthians (1 Cor 11:23–26) and John's gospel (John 13:1–15) proclaimed on this night shows that Eucharist and service are intimately connected. Unmistakably, on the night before he died, Jesus focused his attention on others. We cannot miss this point; Eucharist is about living with and for others. The ritual of washing feet on Holy Thursday evening profoundly shows us how to live in a deeply selfless way.

The ritual of washing feet reminds the church that Eucharist is a ritual of healing and reconciliation. In this same regard, it is imperative for our understanding to note that on Holy Thursday night, during the ritual of foot washing, in essence, there are no spectators. Although there may be representatives actually getting their feet washed, the entire assembly is involved in this ritual on different levels. During this ritual enactment the assembly meditates on charity and love, for this action points to the profound meaning of eucharistic living. Foot washing, as depicted in John's Gospel, signifies that Eucharist connects us with Jesus' ministry of table companionship, and, at the same time, stirs awareness for a more authentic celebration of the Eucharist throughout the year.[13]

Eucharist, Memory, and Imagination

Memory and imagination are indispensable for grounding us in the hope offered to us in Jesus Christ. The Eucharist, the honored place of shared memories, has everything to do with human experience. It holds the promise of revealing to us the God who shows us who we are, and more important, who we are meant to be. At the same time, we need to continually attain new ways to realize the divine so that we can perceive this future filled with hope. The life of faith depends on imagination or it becomes lifeless. In and through the Eucharist, the church has a unique opportunity to spark the "symbolic imagination," and as Richard Cote writes, "symbols open up new levels of awareness about ourselves and about reality that would otherwise remain hidden. . . . They give us insight into the deeper, transcendent meaning of every created being, human and non-human."[14] To illustrate this point, I am reminded of a man who attended our parish parent catechetical sessions. After spending the year immersed in lectionary-based catechesis with his child, he called me on the phone and said, "I was Lazarus and I never knew it."

This man's liturgical experience demonstrates that the backdrop for this most meaningful ritual memorial and the breaking open of the religious imagination is the liturgical year. From Advent through Easter we are immersed into moments of darkness and light, death and new life. And, with each seasonal repetition we enter into the paschal mystery at a deeper level. As we remember past, unrepeatable events, they become present for us now. In this way, we are reminded time and again of God's action and presence in our lives.

As the Christian story unfolds throughout the liturgical year at every celebration of the Eucharist, we are united with all those who have worshiped the Lord from age to age. At the same time, we encounter Christ through the mind of prophets, disciples, sinners, and saints. Deeply significant, it is the gift and grace of the imagination that guides our vision toward a way of knowing learned in and through the celebration of the Eucharist. It is ultimately through the language of symbol that the deep places of our heart are reached and cause us to wonder what directs our worldview, which ought to be rooted in a "Eucharistic imagination."[15]

Conclusion

The above analysis of the Eucharist holds deep meaning and significant implications for the celebration of First Communion. Children come to know the Lord in the midst of a community of believers who gather on Sunday to give thanks and praise to God. As we will see in the next chapter, one of the most powerful ways to show children who we are as Roman Catholics is to place liturgy at the center of their catechesis, particularly as they prepare to celebrate their First Communion. It is my firm belief that Matthew, the child introduced to you at the opening of this chapter, with all his limitations, learned what it meant to meet the Lord in Holy Communion not only from his family but also from a vibrant parish community who faithfully gathers every Sunday throughout the year of feasts and seasons. In the next chapter we will turn our attention to the ways we can immerse children and families into the mystery of God through liturgical catechesis.

4

Graced Journey of Catechesis

You have asked to have your children baptized. In doing so you are accepting the responsibility of training them in the practice of faith. It will be your duty to bring them up to keep God's commandments as Christ taught us, by loving God and our neighbor.

—Rite of Baptism for Children 39

I began working in pastoral ministry right before the RCIA was mandated for use in the United States in 1988. My parish was part of the diocesan pilot program and therefore had implemented the rite a few years prior to 1988. During this time I was also studying theology, which afforded me the wonderful opportunity to delve into the rites of the church and study the documents of Vatican II. For me, the meaning of being a Catholic Christian was met with deep enthusiasm. Deep connections were also made to my daily life. Paschal mystery, for example, became a reality as my husband and I raised three children, as my mother suffered a long battle with cancer, and ultimately as we gathered to celebrate her entry into new life.

During these years our parish life was strong. My husband was the director of liturgical music, I was the director of the catechumenate, and our children attended the parish school. We had fine priests, a dedicated pastoral staff, and very important, a caring parish community that was, for the most part, well-immersed in adult catechesis. Above all, the parish liturgies were celebrated well and were the center of parish life. In fact, I remember distinctly that when my mother died, our children handled her death fairly well. I credited my children's adjustment to the parish community's support that we experienced in a very powerful way.

In time, I moved on to full-time pastoral ministry. I chose catechetical ministry with children because I was convinced that my rich parish experience and understanding of the RCIA could be used to enhance how we teach children about faith and prepare them for the celebration of sacraments. I knew instinctively that the RCIA was a good model and had rich implications for all catechesis. You can imagine how pleased I was when in 1997 the *General Directory for Catechesis* stated:

> The Magisterium of the Church, throughout these years, has never ceased to exercise its pastoral solicitude for catechesis. Numerous Bishops and Episcopal Conferences in all parts of the world have devoted considerable attention to catechesis by means of catechisms and pastoral guidelines, by promoting the formation of their priests and by encouraging catechetical research. Efforts such as these have proved fruitful and have contributed much to catechetical praxis in the particular Churches. The *Rite of Christian Initiation of Adults*, published on 6 January 1972, has proved especially useful for catechetical renewal. (GDC 3)

The *National Directory for Catechesis* (2005) echoes this same sentiment. It states, "The implementation of the *Rite of*

Christian Initiation of Adults in many dioceses and parishes in the United States has emphasized the need for a catechesis based more directly on the baptismal catechumenate. In this context, catechesis aims to achieve a more integral formation of the person rather than merely to communicate information" (NDC 10).[1]

With the above statements in mind, this chapter explores the idea that catechesis for First Communion essentially takes place beyond the classroom. The chapter assumes good classroom instruction for children; however, it makes the claim that relevant family catechesis is essential. Moreover, it is the parish celebration of the Sunday Eucharist that provides the foundational catechesis for the celebration of First Communion liturgies that are reflective of the great mystery of our faith. In five sections, we will explore possibilities for educating children for First Communion that take us beyond the classroom: "Faith First at Home," "Liturgical Catechesis," "Awakening the Sacramental Imagination," "Parent Meetings That Matter," and "The First Communion Rehearsal."

Faith First at Home[2]

Several years into parish catechetical ministry with children, I developed a vision statement for catechesis that viewed the role of the parish as one that assists parents in their responsibility of forming their children in faith. This was based upon the section of the Rite of Baptism cited at the opening of this chapter: "You have asked to have your children baptized. In doing so you are accepting the responsibility of training them in the practice of faith. It will be your duty to bring them up to keep God's commandments as Christ taught us, by loving God and our neighbor" (Rite of Baptism for Children 39).

While this vision is certainly true for children of all ages, it is particularly applicable for young children. Working with parents of young children, I saw the need to reintroduce the parents to the promises they made at their child's baptism. Therefore, I viewed the catechetical process from a different angle—that of the family.

My vision led to the development of a process called "Faith First at Home." It served as the level-one program designed to strengthen the parents' role as the primary catechists for their children. Noteworthy is the fact that although this program was set up for parents with children in the first grade, at times there were parents of older children who were entering the catechetical process for the first time. We chose not to put into practice what some refer to as "catch-up" classes for children who for one reason or another came into the catechetical process later than first grade. In other words, "Faith First at Home" was to be the first catechetical experience for the family. The goals of this program were to bring parents into conversation about their Catholic faith, to recognize their role in catechesis, and to understand the prominent place the church holds for the family in regard to faith formation.

"Faith First at Home" was a structured and well-organized process intended to take place at home within the family. In this initial program the children did not attend class with their peers. Rather, the parents came to regularly scheduled adult sessions during the course of the year, most of which were strategically scheduled around the seasons of the liturgical year. Initially, each family received a packet of materials and was taught how to use them effectively. Materials included a textbook, lectionary-based materials, a liturgical calendar, and a Mass book.

This initial year in the parish catechetical process, level one, provided the foundation for the celebration of First Communion, which ordinarily took place during the Easter season of the child's second year in the process. While the children would most likely attend classes after the first year, we affirmed the continued guiding role of the parent throughout the catechetical process. Undeniably, the same level of commitment and involvement on the part of parents benefited the children throughout their formative years in irreplaceable ways. We also found that as we promoted parental participation, both the church and the family would be strengthened.

In addition to examining the catechetical materials with the parents during the first session, the distinct concept for this type of catechetical process was explained: the importance of the role of the parents in catechesis, Sunday Mass as the heart of the program, and the source of Catholic identity lying hidden in the feasts and seasons of the liturgical year. We were certainly aware that Mass attendance was at a decline for many. Without any judgment on our part, however, the catechetical process assumed Sunday Mass attendance. Therefore, from the very beginning, we spoke about Mass as being the most important event in the life of the Catholic Christian. In essence, we believed that Sunday Mass was the "text" for preparing the children to receive their First Communion, and everything else we did with the children supported this. Significantly, it was acknowledged that developmentally children learn about religious practice in and through the ritual prayer of the church that includes stories of faith, songs of faith, gestures of faith, and images of faith.

Other parent sessions were devoted to exploring feasts and seasons of the liturgical year. These sessions proved to be very valuable. It was here that I discovered, through their own admission, that many parents never learned or understood the relevance of the cycle of feasts and seasons.

One way we emphasized the importance of the cycle of feasts and seasons was to include an engaging liturgical calendar and lectionary-based, user-friendly materials that were conducive for family discussion. We aimed to show that the glory of the liturgical seasons immerses us in the dynamic reality of God's action and presence among us through his Son, Jesus Christ. Moreover, when families are engaged with the seasons of the liturgical year, an appreciation for Advent is restored. By following the liturgical calendar, parents and children learn to appreciate the season without rushing from one season to the next. This was a useful attempt to help families resist the temptation to begin celebrating Christmas before the actual Christmas season. Opportunities to purchase or make Advent wreaths were provided through the parish. Families were reminded that the Christmas Season begins with the Vigil Mass on Christmas Eve and ends with the Feast of the Baptism of the Lord in January. Connections were also made with regard to the decorations we use, the cards we write, the shopping for presents, the Christmas trees we decorate, and the significance of the lights that adorn our homes. Visual images are very important for the faith formation of children. The idea of having religious images displayed at home was also brought to light.

Similar conversations about the liturgical year revolved around the Lent-Easter Cycle. Noteworthy is the forty-day "retreat" that prepares us to renew our baptismal promises. Reflection on the Lenten readings helped families to understand their participation in the practices of charity, fasting, and prayer. There was a huge effort to help families recognize the high point of the liturgical year—the Easter Triduum. We invited everyone, young and old, to participate in the three days to experience the palpable manifestation of Christ's passion, death, and resurrection, and at the same time recognize our own living out of the paschal mystery. It was my contention that children could experience and learn form the rich images of the Easter Triduum: foot washing, cross adoration, and the rites of Christian initiation, for example, are catechesis at its best.

The materials provided families with the tools to continue learning and reflecting throughout Ordinary Time. In reality, in many cases, this was a year-round process, which hopefully would become a way of life.

Faith First at Home: The Rationale

Very simply, the rationale behind the "Faith First at Home" process is church documents. I have already mentioned the Rite of Baptism for Children, which is filled with motives for involving parents in the faith formation of their children in deeper ways. Another often forgotten document is the 1999 *Our Hearts Were Burning Within Us: A Pastoral Plan for Adult Faith Formation in the United States* (OHWB). OHWB recalls, "the Church wisely and repeatedly insists that adult faith formation is 'essential to who we are and what we do as Church' and must be 'situated not at the periphery of the Church's educational mission but at its center'" (OHWB 42). In this regard, "Faith First at Home" skillfully shifts parish catechetical efforts and recognizes that the education of adults does not diminish the education of children; rather, it enhances it. Moreover, the document specifically recalls family, or home-centered activities. The linchpin of the document with regard to family catechesis is, "There may be no place more significant for catechesis than the family. Family catechesis precedes . . . accompanies and enriches all forms of catechesis—and this applies in any structure or stage of family life" (OHWB 102). In the end, as expressed by Kieran Scott, "No religious tradition can survive without reconnecting the chain of memory. Education has to do with the maintenance of the community through the generations—its preservation and improvement. This maintenance or conservation must assure enough continuity of vision and values to sustain the self-identity of the community."[3]

In addition, the *National Directory for Catechesis* echoes the *General Directory for Catechesis* and acknowledges the importance of family catechesis. It states, "In a certain sense nothing replaces family catechesis, especially for its positive and receptive environment, for the example of adults, and for its first explicit experience and practice of the faith" (NDC 203).

The above examples, drawn from the catechetical documents, demonstrate again the importance of reading and interpreting our church documents as a whole.

Faith First at Home: Success Stories

Although every year was different, "Faith First at Home" was successful for many reasons. Most of all, it laid the groundwork for and strengthened the entire catechetical process. It affected the lives of those involved, namely parents, grandparents, and children. Once, after a session exploring the Mass, a non-Catholic father called and asked how he could become Catholic. And, as cited in the last chapter, there was the story about the father who stated, "I never knew, I was Lazarus!" Diane Condon offered a written reflection on her experience as a parent:

> By going through the first grade program with your child, you will see firsthand how children do not separate "religion" from the rest of their life. My first experience with the *Faith First at Home* program was in the Fall of 2001. Reading stories with my oldest son about Jesus' teachings and lessons on being a Christian inevitably raised questions about terror, bad guys in the world, and good vs. evil. In the shadow of uncertain times, how happy I was that these questions were able to be answered by me. There is no place that children feel happier, safer or more secure than in their own home. It is here that the "lessons" they learn become who they are. . . . I eagerly await the knowing glance that Griffin gives me as he listens to the priest read the same Sunday Gospel that we read together at the kitchen table. My husband has recently had his first religious education "teaching" experience with our third son. He was as proud of Brendan for telling me that it was "ordinary time" as he was when he learned to write his name. Faith is a family tradition . . . not an after-school activity or a subject in school. This program reminds you of that.[4]

Faith First at Home: Rich Benefits

Reflecting on this experience, there are many rewards of this model. Not only does it recognize the parents as the primary catechists, it is effective with any set of materials; it is family-based; it can work in any family structure or economic environment; it can work with children with special needs; it engages the whole family; it turns faith formation into a lived experience; it draws families into parish life; it is intergenerational.

Undoubtedly, the vision of the church is to be in partnership with families, especially in regard to education in faith. As pastoral ministers, it is vitally important to understand this connection. It can be reflected in everything we do. Moreover, a positive relationship with parents can have a lasting impact on families. The key is to help them understand their role as Christian parents. When appropriate, go back to the rite of baptism to remind parents of the profound meaning of that ritual action for the life of the entire family.

In my twelve years' experience with "Faith First at Home," I witnessed a vast improvement in the celebrations of First Communion. I would surmise that this was due, in part, to the renewed understanding about the Mass on the part of the entire family. In general, participation in the liturgy was improved, and there was an appreciation for the Sunday Mass option for celebrating First Communion (chapter 5).

Liturgical Catechesis— Awakening the Sacramental Imagination

A critical element in the above-mentioned program was liturgical catechesis. Liturgical catechesis acknowledges liturgy as a source of catechesis. Significantly, the *Catechism of the Catholic Church* states, "Liturgical catechesis aims to initiate people into the mystery of Christ (mystagogy) by proceeding from the visible to the invisible, from the sign to the thing signified, from the 'sacraments' to the 'mysteries'" (CCC 1075). Liturgical catechesis illustrates the rich interplay between liturgy and catechesis. Catechesis of this kind invites us to savor the sacred prayers, Scripture, ritual, music, and environment.

Liturgical catechesis is one of the most noteworthy practices to emerge into parish life in recent years. As a result of the modern catechetical movement, documented as beginning with the 1971 *General Catechetical Directory*, the 1978 *Sharing the Light of Faith: National Catechetical Directory*, and continuing with the 1997 *General Directory for Catechesis* and 2005 *National Directory for Catechesis*, the relationship between liturgy and catechesis has been reclaimed and strengthened. Certainly, this relationship is most clearly seen in the restored *Rite of Christian Initiation of Adults* (RCIA). For example, catechesis during the catechumenate stage is accommodated to the liturgical year and supported by the Liturgy of the Word (RCIA 75). In addition, the main setting for postbaptismal catechesis or mystagogy is the Sunday Mass (RCIA 247). And, as previously stated, the catechetical directories of 1997 and 2005 claim that the RCIA ought to be the model for all catechesis.

According to Gilbert Ostdiek, there are two forms of liturgical catechesis that are equally important. He writes:

> The first can be called *catechesis through liturgy*. The liturgy itself is a form of catechesis. We learn how to do liturgy through repeated participation in it. More importantly, and on a deeper level, the readings, prayers, and gestures work together over long periods of time to shape our ways of perceiving and living out our lives. . . . The second form of liturgical catechesis can be called *catechesis for liturgy*. As the phrase suggests, the goal of this form of liturgical catechesis is to prepare people to participate in the liturgy. . . . Unlike catechesis through liturgy, this second form of catechesis

focuses deliberately on the liturgy itself . . . it is a reflection on the liturgical rites which seeks to break them open to the understanding of the participants.[5]

Both forms of liturgical catechesis are relevant for education in faith for both parents and their children as the children prepare to celebrate their First Communion. This type of catechesis allows us to ask why we do what we do. It focuses on the ritual symbols and actions that spark the religious imagination so that we can see life with new eyes and hear with the language of the heart, which in the end will help us to abandon literalism, which we have been educated toward, and discover the rich images of God found deep within the stories and prayers of the liturgy.[6]

This form of catechesis affirms *lex orandi, lex credendi*—the way in which we pray shapes our belief. As we prepare to bring children to the eucharistic table for the first time we need to help them begin to develop the sense that sacraments call us to a particular way of being in the world. In other words, receiving Communion is our active response to the mission of the church. Young children can grasp this when the adult community embraces it as well. Furthermore, the adult community is responsible for handing on this rich tradition.

Reflection on the celebration of the Eucharist reaffirms who we are as the baptized as we understand more deeply that in and through the celebration of the Eucharist we gather as the Body of Christ, listen to the Word that transforms us, proclaim our identity through the Creed, say "Amen" to Christ's presence, and essentially go forth to live out what we pray. Ultimately, in and through the celebration of the Eucharist we give praise and thanks to God. This is a lifelong process of learning to "see" God's presence and action in the world. Appropriately, Searle writes, "The importance of this reawakening of the religious imagination goes beyond having better liturgies to what really matters: better living."[7]

Parent Meetings that Matter

It seems to me that with each step in a person's sacramental life, there are gaps in understanding. I am not sure why, but it appears to be the case across the country. One reason might be the inconsistencies of practice that occur from parish to parish and from one diocese to another.

Different styles for both catechesis and liturgy may be appropriate; adults and children, however, would benefit from a more consistent appreciation for lifelong learning in regard to faith and pastoral matters. One example of inconsistency is extreme adaptation of the liturgy, in particular for the celebration of First Communion, and this leads to confusion. In other words, although as stated in the *Directory for Masses With Children,* some adaptation is appropriate at times, the Mass should not be altered or embellished in any way for First Communion.

One way to dispel the confusion for how we celebrate First Communion is to create a spirit for education in faith in the parish. Generate an excitement for praying and learning for all age groups: children, youth, young adults, adults, and senior citizens. Consistent efforts at this will strengthen individual faith, and in turn bring people to worship with an awareness of deep Catholic identity.

Teaching and learning about faith is highly important; it does not, however, have to be a strictly didactic experience (although this is appropriate at times) but rather could be an embrace of education as a graced journey of teaching and learning. In other words, education is a nurturing activity that shapes and reshapes people for living and dying. Such a wide, holistic view offers people valuable lifelong lessons. Maria Harris offers a vision of teaching that is approached as an art form that deeply engages the imagination.[8] Such an artistic perception holds rich implications for learning. For example, just as the sculptor sees an image in a piece of

marble, education in faith opens us up to see endless possibilities for life that transcend our current vision.

With this vision of teaching in mind, we can foster a
stronger sense of sacramentality among the parents of the
children ready to receive their First Communion. Since it is
customary in many places to offer parent meetings, make
such gatherings matter. In other words, parent meetings
ought not present the particulars of First Communion day,
for example, Mass schedules, attire, seating, etc. While these
things are important organizationally, they can be commu-
nicated in other ways. Parent meetings can be opportunities for adult catechesis. Just as the previously mentioned
"Faith First at Home" program invited parents to reflect on
their Catholic faith, the parent meeting held prior to the
celebration of First Communion can focus on the impact
of the celebration of the Eucharist within the parents' own
lives and ultimately within the life of the parish community. Meetings of this sort can aid in a profound process of
rediscovery for the participants.

Allow me to offer a sample of what a meaningful parent
meeting might look like. Excerpts here are from meetings
I presented during the time I served in pastoral ministry.
Note that the time frame for the meeting was only one hour.
To demonstrate the parish's collaboration with regard to
sacraments, several members from the pastoral staff were
involved in the meeting, for example, the director of religious education, parish school principal, and pastor. The
elements for a one-hour meeting included:

- Welcome and Introduction
- Hymn (choose a eucharistic hymn from parish reper-
  toire)
- Opening Prayer
- Reading (example, John 13:1-15)

- Reflection (see sample that follows this list)
- Comments, questions, and discussion
- Closing Prayer

A Sample Reflection for the Meeting Facilitator

The reading we just heard is the same reading we hear proclaimed on Holy Thursday evening at the Mass of the Lord's Supper. This is the evening that marks the end of Lent, when we enter into the celebration of the Easter Triduum. On Holy Thursday we remember what Jesus did, and from this we learn what he asks us to do. So, tonight we reflect on Jesus' invitation to "Do this." The 'this' is celebrating the Eucharist; however, it is essentially about our response to the call to be Eucharist for each other— in other words, to take part in Jesus' mission in the world.

In order to better bring our children to the eucharistic table, each one of us needs to experience in a deeper way what it is that we do when we come to the table. Thus, this meeting is an essential aspect of the church's educational ministry. We can never forget that adult education is the center of this ministry, and your presence here tonight strengthens our parish and the quality and effectiveness of our worship together.

I would like to emphasize the following key points:

- We (the church) take the celebration of sacraments very seriously. Sacraments are actions that deepen our experience of God, and in addition they have something to say about our identity as Catholic Christians.
- Although we are extremely excited about our children celebrating sacraments, it is important to emphasize that first sacraments are not things we watch our children do. First sacraments are about children entering into the sacramental life of the church in a deeper

way. In the case of First Communion, remember the children are joining us at the eucharistic table for the first time—and this is a big deal! How we celebrate the liturgy for First Communion reflects this.

- The context of your child's preparation for First Communion is threefold: family, parish community, and education. First, the role of the **family** never loses its significance. Remember, the church recognized the family as the "domestic church." This is a rich, thought-provoking metaphor that merits our attention. It makes it clear that families are sacred and holy. Families have an important role in the church and in the world. They exist for the common good. In families children learn what it means to be caring, loving human beings. In addition, in Christian families, children learn to live within the church culture—they learn a gospel way of life. In teaching children to be faith-filled, the family has the greatest influence. Second to the family is the parish **community**. The worshipping community teaches children week after week what it means to be a baptized member of the church, what it means to be in communion with one another, and what it means to be one with Christ. The parish community is a community rooted in love—it is the reality of Christian life, and we express this in and through sacraments. Third, **education** that is religious is a life-long process that nurtures, forms, shapes, and fashions our lives, our family, and our communities. The educational ministry of our parish through our school and catechetical programs is committed to assisting you in your responsibility of forming your child in faith.[9]

Let us now focus our attention on the sacrament of the Eucharist and look at what it means in our own lives and in the life of the church. This is an opportunity for all of us to experience the Eucharist in a new way; it is a way for us to overcome any limited perception we may have and discover deeper meaning in what we do when we come to celebrate the Eucharist.

Suggestions for Meetings

After such a reflection, the facilitator might offer suggestions for exploring the Eucharist, perhaps asking participants to share some thoughts about their own First Communion experience and how that experience has changed for them as they have grown into adulthood. This also can be an opportunity for liturgical catechesis.

The facilitator can reflect on the Mass and provide some brief insight about, for example, the entrance hymn, the procession, the introductory rites, the liturgy of the Word, the liturgy of the Eucharist, the Communion procession, gestures in the Mass, and the dismissal rite. I once presented a reflection on the introductory rite and spoke about the impact the opening prayer has for me. I shared with the group of parents that as the priest says the words, "Let us pray," I think about how I feel that day—what I bring to this holy place. Another time I mentioned briefly that the Eucharist is the only repeatable sacrament of initiation. Years later a woman told me she had never heard that Eucharist was the only repeatable sacrament of initiation, but she told me that she would never forget it.

Parent meetings need to be planned around the needs of the parish community— meeting people where they are on their spiritual journey without being judgmental or condescending. The importance of this kind of attitude became clear to me over fifteen years ago, when a woman came to me inquiring about becoming a catechist. I naturally asked her what inspired her desire to take part in this ministry. Her response captured my attention and affirmed for me my style of leadership. She said, "For years I attended parent meetings and sat in back because I felt uncomfortable because I never attended Sunday Mass. But you never judged me! I learned many things from you and now I go to Mass every day."

In my experience this style of parent meeting engaged parents more deeply in the catechetical process and ultimately more deeply in their own Catholic faith. They gained renewed awareness that they should not depend entirely on others to teach their children, but rather, they discovered their need to acquire the "tools" to make formation in faith part of their everyday life. It should be noted that the parent meeting addressing the Eucharist was a second parent session. The first was on the often-misunderstood sacrament of reconciliation.

The First Communion Rehearsal

For organizational purposes, especially if you are dealing with large groups of children, a scheduled time to review the First Communion liturgy may be helpful. If done well, this can serve as a means to dispel anxiety for the children and also serve as additional catechesis for the family. Rehearsals can be scheduled for each group (if you have more than one Mass for First Communion), and it is helpful if rehearsals take place in the same space that the First Communion liturgy will take place, presumably the church building.

If you assign seats for families, ask them to sit in the designated seats for this session. Welcome everyone, especially the children, and explain how excited the entire parish is that they will be joining us at the eucharistic table for the first time. If necessary, explain the seating arrangements for families and guests. If you will have a liturgy program or booklet for the occasion, show it and reiterate the importance of participation in the liturgy and gently remind families that the Mass for First Communion is primarily about coming together to pray.

If the children (and maybe the parents) will walk in the entrance procession, rehearse it. Remind the children how to fold their hands and recall that this is our way of saying, "Here I am, Lord." Talk about the significance of the procession; it is essentially the prayer that gathers us, and the families and children are honored to be a part of it on this day. If you include a renewal of baptismal promises or a sprinkling rite on First Communion Day, it may be beneficial to review its connection with the Easter Vigil.

It may not be necessary to go through every part of the Mass since this has been part of the catechesis toward First Communion; however, since it is our goal to bring these families to a profound sense of celebration, it may be helpful to offer some subtle reminders due to the possible distractions of the day. You may point out the importance of listening attentively to the readings and singing the responsorial psalm. Remind them to be alert to posture and gesture, for example, and to pay attention to the times to sit, kneel, and stand.

Some adults and children may take part in the procession of the gifts. This is a good opportunity to explain that all of us have an important role in the Mass as the assembly; at times, representatives are asked to carry out a particular role, for example, bringing the gifts of bread and wine to the altar. Explain that while some people are in this procession, all of us should be mindful that we too are presenting ourselves as gifts to God. This is a good time to reaffirm that at liturgy no one is a spectator. As the assembly we all participate in an extraordinary way.

Take time at the rehearsal to remind this group about the importance of the Eucharistic Prayer. Even if this was discussed (and hopefully it was) during other catechetical sessions for parents, say again that this prayer is the "high point of the entire celebration" (GIRM 30). And, as Barry Hudock affirms, "The eucharistic prayer is *the central and definite liturgical expression of the church's faith.*"[10] In other words, it is creedal! Most important, people need to hear that *we all* pray this prayer.[11]

It is always a good idea to review the procedure for the distribution of Communion. It is preferable for the first communicants to process and receive Communion with the assembly rather than before or separate from the assembly. This practice often comes as a surprise to many, but liturgically and theologically it is appropriate. An explanation may be warranted here regarding the significance of this in the child's life and in the life of the church. The first communicants, as baptized members of the Body of Christ, now *join* us in receiving the Body and Blood of Christ. In addition, it is helpful to remind everyone about reverent gestures. In the United States, it is the norm to receive Holy Communion standing (GIRM 160). There is, however, a particular way to walk in procession: hands folded in prayer, unhurriedly, and preferably in song. Before receiving Communion, the communicant bows his or her head and may receive in the hand or on the tongue (GIRM 160). Note: the question whether the child receives in the hand or on the tongue is a matter of preference. Experience shows, in many cases, it is helpful to depend upon parents for this decision. After receiving Communion, the communicant folds his or her hands while processing unhurriedly back to his or her place.

The question very often arises, "What do the children do when they return to their seats after receiving Communion?" The answer is simple, we sing the Communion hymn! We still have some work to do in regard to why we sing at Mass in general; however, singing during Communion does not diminish our thanksgiving and adoration, but rather enhances it. Chapter 5 will further explore the important issue of music in liturgy with children.

In regard to receiving Communion, care should always be taken to be sensitive to parents who are not Catholic. Let them know that they are welcome, on this day, to come forward with their child (just as they did at the child's baptism) but not to receive Communion.

As the rehearsal draws to a close, discuss the parish policy for taking photos. In many cases, this may be a delicate issue. Many readers may have experienced times when taking photos and videos has gotten out of hand and disrupted the liturgy. As a rule of thumb, you might suggest that photos and videos may be taken only from one's seat; that no photos or videos may be taken during the reception of Communion; and that no professional photographers or videographers will be allowed. It may also be worth noting that once a person clicks a camera, they become disengaged from the prayer. In addition, preoccupation with cameras and other devices actually makes one miss out on the event. In short, it is best to hold the memory in one's heart! After Mass create an opportunity for photos to be taken, perhaps with the priest and other children, with the permission and direction of the pastoral team.

Conclusion

Developing a catechetical plan for families of children ready to receive First Communion is a worthwhile parish venture. It demonstrates the care we have, not only for the liturgical life of the parish, but also for children and families. The suggestions above for a catechetical process, parent meeting, and even the rehearsal stem from the organizational principle in the church that adult catechesis is the axis around which every other form of catechesis swings. This, in my experience, has tremendous implications and transforming effects on an entire parish. Bear in mind, that essentially the entire parish catechizes. In this regard, a "converted" people who understand the need to ritually celebrate Christian life will provide better hope for the children.

Without a doubt, good classroom instruction in faith is vital; this chapter also suggests that other methods that take us beyond the classroom are not only highly effective but also indispensable for the life of the parish. Awareness of multiple forms of education sheds light on a deeper, wider experience. Moreover, the history of education shows us that children learn through traditional family patterns, religious doctrines, and rituals.[12] In describing education that is religious, Gabriel Moran concentrates on four basic social forms that cut across the lifespan and influence all stages of life: family, classroom, job, and leisure.[13] These forms exist in relationship to each other: family is united with community, classroom with knowledge, job with work, and leisure with wisdom. Thus, education is a movement toward community, knowledge, work, and wisdom.[14] Although each form takes on importance at different times during an individual's life, each continues to be a part of the dynamic of human life. In and through these experiences, education discloses meaning and nourishes one's vision for future possibilities.

The educational ministry of the church is in the midst of a paradigm shift, and in the process, religious educators are embracing more and more the practices that foster lifelong learning. When this is a reality, the educational work of the church supports the interplay of the life forms proposed by Moran. An educational process that supports this broader vision is intrinsic to the liturgical life of the parish. The next and final chapter of this book looks to the preparation of the liturgy for First Communion. It explores many realistic, practical aspects to be considered by pastors, religious educators, and liturgy committees.

5

Preparing the Liturgy for First Communion

*As does any art form, the liturgy gives enlarged room
for imagination, for investment in and appropriation
of values, and for freedom. The difference between a
liturgy which does this and one which does not is the
difference between art and propaganda.*

—Aidan Kavanagh[1]

Chapters 1 through 4 provided the liturgical, theological,
and educational framework for considering a pastoral practice for preparing First Communion liturgies. Like the previous chapters, this final chapter is the culmination of years
of pastoral experience integrated with theological, liturgical,
and educational scholarship. The content of this chapter
aims to provide the reader with a hopeful approach for
bringing children to the eucharistic table for the first time.

The celebration of First Communion is a wellspring of
grace and source of renewal for children, families, and the
entire parish community, but it is sometimes problematic

with regard to honoring best liturgical practice. The problem may be due in part to the reality that Masses for First Communion are often completely divorced from the liturgical life of the parish. In many cases, and this is just an observation not a judgment, First Communion resembles more of a classroom scenario, a music recital, or a spectator sport complete with the latest technology for capturing the moment, rather than the celebration of a deeply religious ritual.

The real difficulty in preparing Masses for First Communion may be, as Paul Turner writes, "Rome never authorized a rite for First Communion. The entire custom spread from personal experiences."[2] Regarding other sacraments, for example, baptism and confirmation, there are rites of the church that are followed unquestionably. In addition, many dioceses provide parishes with the appropriate strategy for preparing these rites. In my experience, it appears that no one is willing to disrupt some of the inapt traditions that have become part of the practice of First Communion. I am not entirely sure why not; perhaps it may be partially due to people's expectations. If this is the case, parishes may need to alert people, particularly parents, that the parish desires to be true to the church's liturgical guidelines when preparing the liturgy for First Communion. Therefore, their child's First Communion may not "look" like their own First Communion or the First Communion of an older child. This shift does not in any way diminish the importance of the celebration, but rather enhances the depth of the experience.

Another issue in regard to preparing First Communion liturgies is that the *Directory for Masses With Children*, a document designed to lead preadolescent children to better participation with the adult assembly, has been, for the most part, misinterpreted or ignored (chapter 1).

As previously noted, the first point to consider when preparing the liturgy for First Communion is its context—the celebration of the Eucharist within the parish community (chapter 3). The starting point then is to recognize that First Communion is a parish liturgy. Therefore, the First Communion liturgy, like all sacramental celebrations, needs to be understood within the context of the parish community of faith. In this regard, there are many questions to consider, such as: Do children celebrate First Communion with their class? Do we separate parish schoolchildren from those who attend the parish catechetical program? When do we schedule First Communion liturgies? Do we celebrate First Communion at Sunday Mass? How do we choose the music? How do we select the readers? How do we select the gift bearers? How do we assign seating? Who participates in the entrance procession? How do we facilitate the reception of Communion? With so many questions, it is wise to explore how to make appropriate decisions when preparing the liturgy for the celebration of First Communion.

Many fine materials are available that address meaningful First Communion liturgies. Nevertheless, the starting point to resolving many of these issues is a thorough understanding of the liturgical theology expressed in the Constitution on the Sacred Liturgy (*Sacrosanctum Concilium*). The next step is consultation with the *General Instruction of the Roman Missal,* and as we have already seen in chapter 1, the guide for adaptation—the *Directory for Masses with Children*. In addition, keep in mind the wisdom gained from the *Rite of Christian Initiation of Adults* (RCIA). Ultimately, the key to preparing First Communion liturgies that matter is deep reflection and imaginative interpretation that gets to the heart of pastoral and sacramental theology.

This chapter will explore some of the prevalent questions that surround First Communion liturgies in the following major sections: "Inspiration from the Documents," "Scheduling First Communion Liturgies," "First Communion in the Midst of the Community," "First Communion Outside of Sunday Mass," and "Special Issues to Consider."

Inspiration from the Documents

At times, the last resource you might consider when planning the liturgy for First Communion is the liturgy documents. The mere mention of the word "document" might send shivers down your spine. The documents are not as intimidating as you might think. You may be surprised to find a wellspring of inspiring words that profoundly relate to our Catholic Christian identity.

In chapter 2, it was noted that *Sacrosanctum Concilium* brought forth a renewed theology of the sacraments. This is extremely relevant to our discussion on First Communion liturgies. Adding to this important insight, Rita Ferrone aptly notes, "The Constitution on the Sacred Liturgy stands at the head of all the work of the council—not only chronologically, but also as a sign and symbol of the values and priorities of that council."[3] It is this document, then, that introduces us to several key concepts that are at the heart of liturgy, for example, paschal mystery (SC 2); full, active, and conscious participation (SC 14); liturgical catechesis (SC 33); liturgical ministries (SC 29); and very important, liturgy, the source and summit of the church's life (SC 10).[4] These concepts, among others, lend to the richness of all teaching, learning, and celebrating of our faith. They mark, in a distinct way, the direction we need to take in guiding others toward the celebration of the Eucharist and beyond.

As noted above, the dilemma associated with preparing for the liturgy for First Communion might be that no rite for First Communion exists. We do, however, have the rite of Mass, thus nothing more is needed to prepare the liturgy for First Communion.

Experience shows that one of the pitfalls with regard to First Communion liturgies is that they are planned independently from other parish liturgies. It may be good parish practice for those charged with preparing the liturgy for First

Communion to be appointed to the parish liturgy committee. In this way, First Communion liturgies will reflect the same liturgical principles that go into preparing the Sunday celebration of the Eucharist and other feasts of the liturgical year. In this regard, First Communion is an important aspect of the Easter Season, and the parish would benefit greatly from it if it is planned from this perspective.

The most recent guide for liturgy planning is the *General Instruction on the Roman Missal* (GIRM, 2011), which reflects the *Third Edition of the Roman Missal*, the official translation of the Mass for the English-speaking world. The GIRM affirms much of what has been reflected upon in this book already. For example, it aptly states, "So, in the new Missal the rule of prayer (*lex orandi*) of the Church corresponds to her perennial rule of faith (*lex credendi*), by which we are truly taught that the sacrifice of his Cross and its sacramental renewal in the Mass, which Christ the Lord instituted at the Last Supper and commanded his Apostles to do in his memory, are one and the same, differing only in the manner of their offering; and as a result, that the Mass is at one and the same time a sacrifice of praise, thanksgiving, propitiation, and satisfaction" (GIRM 3).

This being said, we need to offer children no less than the profound mystery found in the prayers of the Mass. Keep in mind that children do not have to understand, in a cognitive way, every word that is prayed. But rather, they need to be exposed to the prayer of the church, which expresses the profound tradition of which they are a part. For, as Sofia Cavalletti writes, "In the religious sphere, it is a fact that children know things no one has told them."[5] Moreover, adults can learn from children when they take the time to reflect and talk with children about their religious experiences.

In addition, Thomas Shepard makes some important points regarding children and liturgy. He writes, "Children need ritual. It helps reassure them about their environment and about what is true and false. That's important to remember, because sometimes well-meaning adults change the ritual every time they gather . . ."[6] Children therefore need to experience the Mass authentically. Chapter 1 explored some of the general principles for understanding liturgy with children that are helpful to those who prepare First Communion liturgies. Additionally, it is indispensable when those who prepare First Communion liturgies are well-versed in the principles spelled out in the GIRM. In turn, pastoral adaptations may be arranged on occasion. These adaptations are reflected in the *Directory for Masses With Children.*

In chapter 1 we looked at some of the key themes of the *Directory for Masses With Children* (DMC). As previously stated, the DMC cannot be read in isolation because adaptation is appropriate only when measured against the principles of the GIRM (as well as other liturgical documents). For example, in chapter 2, section 3 of the GIRM, "The Individual Parts of the Mass" is extremely helpful when preparing First Communion liturgies. This section is a catechetical gem that uncovers the principles of our rich tradition and its expression in our time. Immersion into the depth of the prayer of the church helps us to make better decisions when celebrating the liturgy for the special occasion of First Communion.

An example of this view may assist here. During a particular First Communion liturgy, the priest-celebrant remained in the center aisle after the completion of the entrance hymn. He then proceeded to casually speak to the children, one by one. However, the GIRM is clear: "When the Entrance Chant is concluded, the Priest stands at the chair and, together with the whole gathering, signs himself with the Sign of the Cross. Then by means of the Greeting he signifies the presence of the Lord to the assembled community. By this greeting and the people's response, the mystery of the Church gathered together is made manifest. After the greeting of the people, the Priest, or the Deacon, or a lay minister may very briefly introduce the faithful to the Mass of the Day" (GIRM 50). Very simply, then, the priest might have honored the direction, and after the sign of the cross and proper greeting of the people, acknowledged the presence of the first communicants. This may seem finicky, but to avoid confusion, it is important to maintain the ritual prayer of the church.[7]

The example above demonstrates that many well-intentioned adults attempt to change the ritual in an effort to make it "special." Experience confirms that children who participate in the Sunday Eucharist with their family on a consistent basis will undoubtedly understand that when they approach the altar to receive Holy Communion *with* the assembly, it is extraordinarily special! If we perpetuate a false sense of uniqueness in the First Communion liturgy, we risk the children remembering those actions that are not significant to this profound event.

Before exploring practical ideas for preparing the First Communion liturgy, let us first look at another important influence for good practice. In addition to the church's guidelines for preparing liturgy, in view of the reality that First Communion is fundamentally about Christian initiation, we can also look to the *Rite of Christian Initiation of Adults* (RCIA) for wisdom when bringing children to the eucharistic table for the first time.

Clearly, it is not my intention to imply that we should use the rites of Christian initiation, as such, for they are intended exclusively for the unbaptized seeking full initiation into the church, or for those from other ecclesial communities seeking full communion with the Catholic Church. However, embedded within the rites of initiation are subtle hints for what we can do as we welcome children to the table to receive Communion for the first time.

As we have seen throughout this book, the RCIA has many implications for celebrating First Communion. Here we will discover some implications for how we envision the liturgy for First Communion. Take for example Part II of the RCIA, "Christian Initiation of Children Who Have Reached Catechetical Age." Although intended for use with children not baptized as infants, it is applicable to celebrating liturgy with baptized children. Furthermore, experience with children in the catechumenate demonstrates that they are able to connect Word and sacrament to their lives. It is therefore very helpful for preparers of the liturgy to understand the RCIA and its impact on the entire parish. In other words, the RCIA should not be viewed as another parish activity listed in the parish bulletin. It should be understood and appreciated more like a wave that washes up on the shores of parish life, transforming it forever. The RCIA teaches us that ministry with children should primarily be initiatory and formational. Ultimately, the goal is to initiate children into the liturgical life of the church.

We Celebrate the Eucharist, a best-selling text, provides a model for eucharistic catechesis based upon the wisdom of the RCIA. Significantly, it emphasizes the importance of the parish community, invites children and parents to engage in a step-by-step process or journey of faith, and unfolds the mystery of the Eucharist throughout the process by way of various ritual celebrations. The program explores the meaning of baptism, the parts of the Mass, ministries in the church, and preparation for Mass, and highlights the importance of *mystagogy*.[8] Let us not forget, after the children have celebrated their First Communion, it is very effective to allow them to share their experience, and in doing so they uncover the meaning of Eucharist in their lives.

The RCIA provides us with yet another thought-provoking message with regard to the celebration of First Communion. Currently, for historical reasons, we associate the reception of First Communion with age seven, or the second grade in school. Perhaps we might begin to think more about a readiness model that is not entirely associated with a particular age or grade level.

To illustrate, I recall two experiences. During my first year in pastoral ministry, a parent of a child in our level-two class expressed the desire that her child not participate in the parish celebration of First Communion because, in her experience, the celebration of First Communion presented too many distractions from what was actually important. She asked if her child could receive at the Christmas Midnight Mass in which the entire family would be present. I agreed, first because I respected the parent and what she considered best for her child, and second, the child was ready. On another occasion, a parent approached the pastor and asked if her child, who had just completed the first grade, could receive his First Communion without delay. The parent was confident that the child was ready. The pastor spoke with me, and we agreed that this was an ideal situation mainly because the parent came to the church requesting this sacrament for her son in the same way she did for his baptism. After a delightful meeting with the parent and the child, the parish celebrated the child's First Communion at a Sunday Mass in July. In both situations it was evident that Sunday Eucharist was an important part of the two families' lives. Be aware that in such cases, parish administrators need to be attentive to proper record keeping.

Scheduling First Communion Liturgies

Many people often associate First Communion with the month of May. This may be due, in part, to evidence that the ritualization of First Communion, beginning in 1593, occurred during a time in the church when devotions of many kinds developed in the church. Paramount among these was devotion to the Blessed Mother. Peter McGrail notes that the early French model for celebrating First Communion included, in addition to a renewal of baptismal promises, a consecration to the Virgin Mary.[9] There is nothing inappropriate with this, and, in fact, it is admirable. Moreover, the church's contemporary understanding of sacraments incorporates such devotion but moves beyond it.

Eucharist, as previously noted, is a sacrament of initiation. It is an action of the church that incorporates us more deeply into the Body of Christ. Additionally, the sacraments of initiation are best understood as Easter sacraments, that is, they signify new life in Christ. With this in mind, scheduling First Communion liturgies during the Easter Season is most appropriate. In this way, just as we do with the elect, connections can be made with Lent, the Triduum, and Easter. Keep in mind, then, depending on the date of Easter Sunday, First Communion may take place in the month of April. In my pastoral experience, although we always scheduled First Communion in the first weeks of the Easter season, it surprised many when April dates were announced. Therefore, education on the significance of the Easter sacraments may be warranted.

First Communion in the Midst of the Community

During the past fifty years or so, there has been much debate in many places regarding celebrating First Communion during the regularly scheduled parish Sunday Masses. Most likely we have all experienced stories about the regular Mass attendees' complaints about forfeiting their seats, or the additional time it takes when a special event takes place at Mass. It is not a new concept that First Communion be celebrated in the midst of the community because the Sunday assembly, the gathering of the baptized, is the initiating community. This is a significant ideal recovered with the restoration of the rites of Christian initiation. The RCIA states, "The initiation of catechumens is a gradual process that takes place within the community of the faithful" (RCIA 4). In the same manner, then, the initiation of baptized children should take place within the community of the faithful.

The depth of this understanding comes from the reality that we are called by God to participate in the Sunday assembly. As Anne Koester points out, "There's a choice to make each Sunday: . . . to go or not to go to Mass. We have a standing invitation to participate in Sunday worship. Who invites us? God does. God invites, and as with all invitations a response follows. By choosing to come on Sundays—to be part of the church assembled for worship—we respond positively to God's invitation."[10] This invitation begins with baptism, the sacrament of initiation that calls us into relationship with Christ and with one another. The latter point is often missed. If we really recognize that we are in relationship with each other, we might realize that we are also called to support others as they respond to God's call, especially in and through the sacraments. This profound understanding of who we are as a worshipping community undeniably adds vitality and great potential to the parish.

This ideal can be reached rather simply. The following practices for celebrating First Communion at a Sunday Mass are suggestions that work in both small and large parishes:

- Plan in advance at which Masses First Communion will be celebrated and announce it in the parish bulletin.

- Give families a choice about which Mass they would like for their child to receive First Communion.

- Limit to ten, depending on the size of your parish, the number of first communicants at a given Mass.

- Reserve a row in a prominent place in the assembly for each communicant's family.
- Maintain the Easter decorations for First Communion liturgies.

The key to the success of celebrating First Communion at Sunday Mass is that no additional, unnecessary practices are added. The addition of needless practices was common in the 1970s and 1980s due in part to the misinterpretation of adaptation in the liturgy; in some cases inappropriate practices still remain. For example, children need not be expected to become the liturgical ministers, perform a special song, or ritually accept their First Communion certificate. In addition, the procession of gifts should not be embellished with symbolic gifts accompanied by explanation in an effort to involve several children.

The key to the assembly's appreciation for bringing first communicants to the Sunday Mass is a well-celebrated parish liturgy where everyone is engaged faithfully in the prayer of the church. It may be appropriate for some of the children to bring up the gifts. Here again, we can gain some wisdom from the RCIA. "Third Step: Celebration of the Sacraments of Initiation" (RCIA 241) states, "Some of the neophytes also take part in the procession to the altar with gifts." This statement tells us that the newly initiated need not participate in the Mass beyond their role as active participants in the liturgy—as members of the assembly. With this in mind, consider the following when planning to celebrate First Communion at Sunday Mass:

- Children, and possibly their parents, may take part in the opening procession.
- Children and their families may be seated in a reserved section of the assembly.

- After the greeting of the people, when introducing the faithful to the Mass of the day (GIRM 50), the priest may acknowledge the presence of the children celebrating their First Communion and remind the assembly of their role in the Christian initiation of these children.

- Children may renew their baptismal promises with the assembly, or the liturgy could include a sprinkling rite.

- Children should not be the readers of Scripture or the intercessions. This role should be reserved for the commissioned reader.

- Homilies should reflect the Scripture readings, while at the same time connecting with the occasion, and should avoid watered-down eucharistic theology, the asking of questions, or any type of gimmick.

- Some children *may* participate in the procession of gifts to the altar, but catechesis prior to First Communion should emphasize the symbolic nature of this action, that is, no one is a spectator and in essence we all bring forth our gifts (GIRM 73).

- The procession of gifts should include bread and wine only; symbolic gifts are never appropriate.

- Children should be part of the Communion procession, receiving Communion under both species *with* the other members of the assembly (receiving the wine should be at the discretion of the parents).

- Before saying "This is the Lamb of God," the celebrant may remind the assembly of the "preeminence of the eucharist" (RCIA 243).

- After the Prayer after Communion, before the dismissal rite, the priest may ask the assembly to acknowledge with brief applause the children who received their First Communion.

- Maintaining regulations regarding photo taking and videography will help keep the focus on the liturgy and prevent distractions. Ideally there should be no photo taking at Mass, particularly during the reception of Communion. Announce ahead of the day when and where the opportunities for photo taking after Mass will be, and inform families to avoid hiring photographers or videographers.

Some parishes may take the ideal of Sunday First Communion very seriously and have first communicants present at every Sunday Mass during the Easter Season. For pastoral reasons, other parishes may wish to designate Masses at other times for this purpose. When this is the case, attention to liturgical principles is paramount.

First Communion Outside of Sunday Mass

For various pastoral reasons, First Communion is often celebrated outside of Sunday Mass, perhaps on a Saturday morning or afternoon. Great care needs to be taken to ensure that the same principles for Sunday Mass are applied in the preparations. In very large parishes there may be more than three hundred children for First Communion. Therefore, a fair amount of coordination is necessary. While most of the suggestions cited above for Sunday Masses are applicable, the following practices should be considered:

- If you regularly have a Mass for Families in your parish, use this as a model for preparing First Communion liturgies.
- To avoid overcrowding, schedule as many as eight Masses over two or three weeks during the Easter season.
- In order to keep the numbers manageable, allow families to "register" well in advance for a particular Mass.

- Also, consider designating several Sunday Masses during the Easter season for the celebration of First Communion; allow families to select this option.
- Avoid assigning children to a particular celebration by their class in school.
- Avoid separating children who attend the parish school from those who participate in the parish catechetical program; these liturgies should always promote a sense of a parish celebration.
- Do not separate first communicants from their families.
- Choose music from the repertoire sung at Sunday Mass.
- Schedule parish lectors; if your parish has commissioned youth or young adults for this ministry, you might tap into this group.
- Schedule extra parish Extraordinary Ministers of Holy Communion to accommodate large Mass attendance.
- Follow appropriate liturgical practice; do not use this occasion for allowing inappropriate practices.

Special Issues to Consider

Some of the suggestions above warrant further explanation. Very often, conflict arises regarding how parishes approach the celebration of First Communion with the children who attend the parish school versus those who attend the parish catechetical program. Sadly, it remains the practice in many parishes that First Communion liturgies are celebrated separately for children in the parish school. This is not good practice for the simple reason that sacraments are parish celebrations. And any separation of children by virtue of where they go to school essentially compromises the church's mission. This practice also raises a larger question as to whether those involved with the parish school view themselves as part of the parish community or school community. If this is the case, efforts can be made to instill a stronger sense of parish community where authentic opportunities for families to come together in different ways can be created long before the celebration of First Communion. One way to do this might be to invite these groups to come together for a particular Sunday Mass on a monthly basis prior to First Communion. The parish can also pray for all children in the prayer of the faithful during the time of their immediate preparation for First Communion. Ultimately, all parish families should experience a deep sense of hospitality and be thoroughly convinced that the children preparing for First Communion belong to the parish. The rationale for such efforts can be found in the *Catechism of the Catholic Church*. It states:

> "A *parish* is a definite community of the Christian faithful established on a stable basis within a particular church; the pastoral care of the parish is entrusted to a pastor as its own shepherd under the authority of the diocesan bishop."* It is the place where all the faithful can be gathered together for the Sunday celebration of the Eucharist. The parish initiates the Christian people into the ordinary expression of the liturgical life: it gathers them together in this celebration; it teaches Christ's saving doctrine; it practices the charity of the Lord in good works and brotherly love. (CCC 2179;* the quote within this quote is from CCL 515 §1)

Organizational change may be considered in some places due to a particular culture that has persisted for a long time. Significantly, change involves meaningful transformation. The strength, wisdom, and vision of a parish can bring about meaningful change when the pastoral staff, volunteers, and the faithful work together and embrace the vision of the church in combination with the good of the entire community. A healthy parish mission and vision will undoubtedly contribute to eloquent First Communion liturgies.

To maintain a sense of an assembly at prayer, the seating of the first communicants is another issue that strikes me as a topic worth reflecting on. For well over thirty years, in most parishes, children have been seated with their parents and families during the Mass for First Communion. Reasons for this were cited in chapter 1's discussion on the *Directory for Masses With Children*. Remember, after Vatican II, the movement from separating children from their parents for liturgy had to do with the important role of the parents in the life of their children.

In recent years there has been some setback. Many parishes are separating children from their families at First Communion. Reasons for this practice are in response to justifiable concerns regarding distractions when children are with their family. Experience shows that many fear the children will not participate well in the company of their parents and family. If this is the case, parent education, as explored in the last chapter, will help dissipate this situation. Believe it or not, seating arrangements reflect our theology of the Body of Christ. In addition, separating children from their family for the celebration of First Communion, in practice, creates a situation that places the adults as spectators and puts the children on display. The liturgy becomes child-centered rather than the assembly gathered in prayer to celebrate this wonderful event in the life of the children, the family, and the church. In order to create a sense of mutuality, some parishes even go as far as not having any special seating for the First Communion liturgy. Children and families assemble as they would for Sunday Mass throughout the year. There is merit here worth considering.

A final area of concern in regard to preparing First Communion liturgies is music. In addition to working collaboratively with the parish music director, those who prepare the liturgy for First Communion should be familiar with *Sing to the Lord: Music in Catholic Worship* (STL), a revision of earlier documents on liturgical music, approved for use in 2007. Like the other documents cited above, STL is to be used in used in conjunction with the *General Instruction of the Roman Missal*.

There is no better way to evoke the religious imagination than through music. Music is prayer and is never meant to be a distraction (DMC 32) or entertainment. Its place in the liturgy has profound meaning. Notably, STL states, "A cry from deep within our being, music is a way for God to lead us to the realm of higher things. As St. Augustine says, 'Singing is for the one who loves.' Music is therefore a sign of God's love for us and of our love for him" (STL 2).

Meaningfully, Thomas Shepard makes the claim, "But children have a special affinity for music. They are so open to it that you can often teach them with greater ease than you can adults. . . . Lyrics are important, but if the words are sometimes obscure, don't worry. Children don't have to know the meaning of every single word. Music is basically emotion—not an exercise of the mind, but a calling forth of a feeling."[11] In other words, when choosing music for First Communion, choose the same music that you would for other parish liturgies, appropriate to the liturgical season, presumably Easter. In this way children and families will be familiar with the hymns and responses. In addition, the singing of hymns can be an important part of the child's formation in faith, at home and in class.

Conclusion

First Communion liturgies impact a child's experience of faith. Therefore, how the parish prepares the liturgy for this occasion matters. In our time so many things are driven by the motive for entertainment, and unfortunately this attitude has found its way into the prayer of the church. No doubt, as pastoral ministers for children and families we have multiple challenges. We may need, however, to be more cautious than creative. We will consistently benefit by stepping back to reflect on what it is we want to teach children and families about Eucharist and receiving Holy Communion for the first time. People are yearning to experience a real sense of hope. We have the "tools." We need only to use them well. Any thoughts of inventing secular themes for First Communion liturgies are not only inappropriate but not the least bit helpful. Liturgy with children and families, particularly First Communion, needs to be connected to the ordinary, with liturgy beckoning us to reach beyond that which is commonplace so that we might "see" the glory of God who loves us first and desires to share life with us.

In other words, liturgy with children should be different from other meaningful experiences such as school graduations, music recitals, and sports events. It must lure them on a profoundly different level. Therefore, trust the liturgy; let the symbols and words speak. Tell the stories of old with a new enthusiasm. Let the homily open new doors of possibility. Allow moments of silence to whisper in each heart, "God is here." Fill the space with music that bathes the assembly with wonder and awe. Help the assembly appreciate the sense that they are gathered together in a unique way. In this way, as the prayer of the church unfolds and the children hear the words "The Body of Christ," "The Blood of Christ," and they respond "Amen" for the first time, they will instinctively know this is Jesus Christ, whose birth we celebrate at Christmas and whose death and resurrection we remember at Easter.

Epilogue:
The Landscape of
First Communion

The chapters of *First Communion Liturgies* are an attempt to "stir up" a deeper consciousness regarding how we prepare and celebrate First Communion liturgies. While some people are under the impression that issues of concern are prevalent only in certain parts of the United States, others are more certain that the uneasiness about inappropriate practices is worldwide.[1]

Many "out of place" practices, or so-called "adaptations," have taught over two generations that these "adaptations" are acceptable, and these are what make the day a special event. In some cases, the liturgy for First Communion extends well beyond two hours and is described as "cute." While many parishes have made strides with minor changes in practice, others have been courageous enough to make the move away from, for example, expensive dresses and suits, clothing the first communicants in white albs, which are reminiscent of the baptismal garment.

Sadly, experience also shows that in many cases, high emotions and sentimentality often resist any change. There is widespread preoccupation with banners, attire, photographers, certificates, and special performances by the children. These practices are not particularly beneficial and take away from the profound event of a child's First Communion. In addition, some catechetical practices encourage a "graduation" mentality, complete with certificates and rewards along the way.

What may be needed is a radical change in catechesis, both toward the celebration of First Communion and beyond. Emphasis should be placed on the profound reality of the child's initiation into the eucharistic life of the church. This profound truth is often missed. For example, a parent's troubling outcry following the final preparations for First Communion Day confirms my suspicion of First Communion being a "spectacle." The parent exclaimed, "This is nothing special; it's just like Sunday Mass!" I am certain, many would agree, there is a deeper issue at stake here; some people do not realize that Sunday Mass is the most important activity of the Catholic Christian community. It is for this reason that I adhere to placing Sunday Eucharist at the center of all catechesis.

A comprehensive, diocesan and parish-wide approach toward catechesis and the celebration of First Communion ought to be considered. The recent trend, in many places, of proving Mass attendance through taking attendance or some sort of "stamp" on the bulletin or other creative gimmicks may have immediate results, but its long-term effects are doubtful. I worry that we are teaching children and families that going to Mass is an assignment, and the celebration of First Communion is the reward. Efforts to restore a sense of the sacred in a secular world, on the other hand, will have long-term effects.

For these efforts to be a consistent reality, pastoral education is key. Pastoral education on matters related to First Communion liturgies has to take place in seminaries, graduate ministerial programs, Catholic schools, and parish catechetical programs for both children and adults.

Education in faith is a nurturing activity that unlocks the religious imagination. It is "openness to the future that is beyond all futures."[2] Ultimately, education is about ongoing transformation, and it can affect the life of the church at deep levels. Take the plunge to reaffirm the value of the Sunday assembly in relation to First Communion liturgies. Imagine a different way of preparing and celebrating First Communion liturgies. Unwrap the profound meaning of this sacrament of initiation for the children, the family, and the parish community, so that, together, in and through the celebration of the Eucharist we will discover the grace and gift of a revealing God.

After more than twenty years of meaningful work in pastoral ministry, I am currently privileged to work in theological (higher) education. Through teaching I have discovered the rich, wide experience I bring to the theoretical. The people that I served in the past, and my colleagues in ministry, inspired the chapters of this book in so many ways. It is my sincere hope that I am able to minister to you, the reader, and inspire you to serve the church well.

Feast of the Baptism of the Lord
January 12, 2014

Notes

Introduction—pages 1–4

1. Frank C. Senn, *Christian Liturgy: Catholic and Evangelical* (Minneapolis: Fortress, 1997), 704.

Chapter 1: Liturgy with Children—pages 5–17

1. See *The Content of Faith: The Best of Karl Rahner's Theological Writings,* ed. Karl Lehmann and Albert Raffelt (New York: Crossroads, 1992), 124.

2. Mark Searle, "Images and Worship," in *Vision: The Scholarly Contributions of Mark Searle to Liturgical Renewal*, ed. Anne Y. Koester and Barbara Searle (Collegeville, MN: Liturgical Press, 2004), 126–37.

3. Richard Cote, *Lazarus! Come Out! Why Faith Needs Imagination* (Ottawa: Novalis, 2003), 9.

4. Gabriel Moran, *Religious Education Development: Images for the Future* (Minneapolis: Winston, 1983), 147.

5. Dwayne Huebner, "The Capacity for Wonder and Education," in *The Lure of the Transcendent: Collected Essays by Dwayne Huebner*, ed. Vikki Hillis (Mahwah, NJ: Lawrence Erlbaum Associates, Publishers, 1999), 3.

6. Mary Collins, "Is the Adult Church Ready for Liturgy with Young Christians?" in *The Sacred Play of Children*, ed. Diane Apostolos-Cappadona (New York: Seabury, 1983), 3–17.

7. See Thomas Shepard, "What Does It Mean to Be a Child?" in *Children, Liturgy, and Music,* ed. Virgil C. Funk (Washington, DC: The Pastoral Press, 1990), 71–77.

8. Huebner, "The Capacity for Wonder and Education," 7.

9. See Gabriel Moran, *Education Towards Adulthood: Religion and Lifelong Learning* (New York: Paulist Press, 1979), chap. 2.

10. See the dedication page in Antoine de Saint-Exupéry, *The Little Prince* (New York: Harcourt Brace, 1943).

11. See Shepard, "What Does It Mean to Be a Child?" 75.

12. Julia Upton, "Personal Obstacles to Ritual Prayer," in *The Renewal That Awaits Us*, ed. Eleanor Bernstein and Martin F. Connell (Chicago: Liturgy Training Publications, 1997), 150–59.

13. Searle, "Images and Worship," 131.

14. This section is adapted from the author's featured article on Praytellblog.com, September 3, 2010.

15. See *General Directory for Catechesis* (Washington, DC: United States Catholic Conference, 1997) and *National Directory for Catechesis* (Washington, DC: United States Conference of Catholic Bishops, 2005).

16. Shepard, "What Does It Mean to Be a Child?" 74.

17. Mark Searle, "Children in the Assembly of the Church," in *Children in the Assembly of the Church*, ed. Eleanor Bernstein and John Brooks-Leonard (Chicago: Liturgy Training Publications, 1992), 30–50.

Chapter 2: Developing Patterns of First Communion— pages 18–33

1. For a more detailed explanation of the history of First Communion see Paul Turner, *Ages of Initiation: The First Two Christian Millennia* (Collegeville, MN: Liturgical Press, 2000); Peter McGrail, *First Communion: Ritual, Church and Popular Religious Identity* (Burlington, VT: Ashgate Publishing Company, 2007); Maxwell E. Johnson, *The Rites of Initiation: Their Evolution and Interpretation* (Collegeville, MN: Liturgical Press, 2007); Edward Yarnold, SJ, *The Awe-Inspiring Rites of Initiation: The Origins of the R.C.I.A.* (Collegeville, MN: Liturgical Press, 1994); Matthew M. Crotty, *The Recipient of First Communion: A Historical Synopsis and Commentary* (Washington, DC: Catholic University of America Press, 1947).

2. Turner, *Ages of Initiation*, 8.

3. Ibid., 7.

4. Paul Turner, *The Hallelujah Highway: A History of the Cate-chumenate* (Chicago: Liturgy Training Publications, 2000), 49.

5. *Egeria's Travels*, 3rd ed., trans. John Wilkinson (Warminster, England: Aris & Phillips, 1999), 58–59.

6. Crotty, *The Recipient of First Communion*, 10.

7. Turner, *Ages of Initiation*, 29–30.

8. See John W. O'Malley, *Trent: What Happened at the Council* (Cambridge, MA: Belknap, 2013).

9. William A. Herr, *This Our Church,* Basics of Christian Thought (Chicago: The Thomas More Press, 1986), 242–43.

10. See O'Malley, 188, 281.

11. Teri Martini, *The Fisherman's Ring: The Life of Saint Pius X, The Children's Pope* (Patterson, NJ: St. Anthony Guild, 1954), 111.

12. See Pope Pius X, *All Things in Christ; Encyclicals and Selected Documents of Saint Pius X*, ed. Vincent A. Yzermans (Westminster, MD: The Newman Press, 1954), 8.

13. See Pope Pius X, *Catechetical Documents of Pope Pius X*, ed. Joseph Burns Collins, (Patterson, NJ: Saint Anthony Guild, 1946).

14. Joseph Dougherty, *From Altar-Throne to Table: The Campaign for Frequent Holy Communion in the Catholic Church* (Lanham, MD: The Scarecrow Press, 2010), 6.

15. Robert Taft, *Beyond East and West: Problems in Liturgical Understanding* (Washington, DC: Pastoral Press, 1984), 105.

16. Dougherty, 105.

17. References to *Quam Singulari* are from Pope Pius X, *All Things in Christ*, 245–50.

18. Paul B. Marx, *Virgil Michel and the Liturgical Movement* (Collegeville, MN: Liturgical Press, 1957), 95.

19. Dougherty, 106.

20. Keith F. Pecklers, *The Unread Vision: The Liturgical Movement in the United States of America 1926–1955* (Collegeville, MN: Liturgical Press, 1998), 11.

21. R. W. Franklin and Robert L. Spaeth, *Virgil Michel American Catholic* (Collegeville, MN: Liturgical Press, 1988), 14, 34.

22. Pecklers, *The Unread Vision*, xiii.

23. Ibid., 25.

24. Reference to the documents of the Second Vatican Council are from *Vatican Council II: The Conciliar and Postconciliar Documents*, trans. Austin Flannery (Collegeville, MN: Liturgical Press, 2014).

25. Turner, *Ages of Initiation,* 38.

26. Ibid., 37, 39.

27. Ibid., 36.

28. McGrail, 12.

29. Ibid., 13.

30. Turner, *Ages of Initiation,* 60.

31. Crotty, 18.

32. Ibid., 19.

33. See Jo-Ann Metzdorff, "The Consumer Culture and Family Faith Formation, Practice and Preparation for First Holy Communion" (DMin thesis, Seminary of the Immaculate Conception, 2007).

Chapter 3: First Communion in Context— pages 34–47

1. Maria Harris, *Fashion Me a People: Curriculum in the Church* (Louisville, KY: Westminster John Knox, 1989), 94.

2. John P. Beal, James A. Coriden, Thomas J. Green, eds., *The New Commentary on the Code of Canon Law: Commissioned by the Canon Law Society of America* (Mahwah, NJ: Paulist Press, 2000), 1108.

3. David Rizzo, *Faith, Family, and Children with Special Needs: How Catholic Parents and their Kids with Special Needs Can Develop a Richer Spiritual Life* (Chicago: Loyola, 2012), 42–43.

4. Kevin Irwin, *Models of the Eucharist* (Mahwah, NJ: Paulist Press, 2005), 20.

5. John D. Laurance, *The Sacrament of the Eucharist*, Lex Orandi (Collegeville, MN: Liturgical Press, 2012), vii.

6. Julia Upton, *A Church for the Next Generation: Sacraments in Transition* (Collegeville, MN: Liturgical Press, 1990), 7.

7. Aidan Kavanagh, *The Shape of Baptism: The Rite of Christian Initiation* (New York: Pueblo, 1978), 122.

8. See Nathan Mitchell, *Meeting Mystery: Liturgy, Worship, Sacraments* (Maryknoll, NY: Orbis, 2006), xiii.

9. Mark Searle, *The Church Speaks About Sacraments with Children: Baptism, Confirmation, Eucharist, Penance* (Chicago: Liturgy Training Publications, 1990), 60.

10. See Enrico Mazza, *Mystagogy: A Theology of Liturgy in the Patristic Age*, trans. Matthew J. O'Connell (New York: Pueblo, 1989).

11. See Massimo Faggioli, *True Reform: Liturgy and Ecclesiology in Sacrosanctum Concilium* (Collegeville, MN: Liturgical Press, 2012).

12. Joseph Cardinal Ratzinger, *God Is Near Us: The Eucharist, The Heart of Life* (San Francisco: Ignatius, 2003), 43.

13. For more on the meaning of the ritual of foot washing on Holy Thursday see Donna M. Eschenauer, *The Easter Triduum: A Ritual Pilgrimage* (San Jose, CA: Resource Publications, 2013).

14. Cote, *Lazarus Come Out*, 40–41.

15. Walter Brueggemann, *The Prophetic Imagination*, 2nd ed. (Minneapolis: Fortress, 2001), xx.

Chapter 4: Graced Journey of Catechesis— pages 48–68

1. According to the United States Conference of Catholic Bishops, references from the 2005 *National Directory for Catechesis* are made to page numbers, not paragraph numbers.

2. The idea to name the parish program "Faith First at Home" was taken from *Faith First at Home*, published by RCL Benziger and no longer in print. In no way does this author imply that other texts cannot be used.

3. Kieran Scott, "Continuity and Change in Religious Education," in *Critical Issues in Religious Education*, Oliver Brennan, ed. (Dublin, Ireland: Veritas, 2005), 79–98.

4. Diane Condon, "Faith First at Home—A Family Tradition," *Ag-neWs,* Spring 2004.

5. Gilbert Ostdiek, *Catechesis for Liturgy: A Program for Parish Involvement* (Washington, DC: Pastoral Press, 1986), 9–10.

6. Mark Searle, "Images and Worship," in *Vision: The Scholarly Contributions of Mark Searle to Liturgical Renewal*, eds. Anne Y. Koester and Barbara Searle (Collegeville, MN: Liturgical Press, 2004), 130.

7. Ibid., 135.

8. See Maria Harris, *Teaching and the Religious Imagination: An Essay in the Theology of Teaching* (San Francisco: HarperCollins, 1987).

9. Also see Thomas Groome, *Will There Be Faith: A New Vision for Educating and Growing Disciples* (New York: HarperCollins, 2011).

10. Barry Hudock, *The Eucharistic Prayer: A User's Guide* (Collegeville, MN: Liturgical Press, 2010), 4.

11. Ibid., 10–19.

12. See Gabriel Moran, *Religious Education as a Second Language* (Birmingham, AL: Religious Education Press, 1989), and *Showing How: The Act of Teaching* (Valley Forge, PA: Trinity Press International, 1997).

13. Moran, *Showing How*, 157.

14. Moran, *Religious Education Development*, 166.

Chapter 5: Preparing the Liturgy for First Communion—pages 69–87

1. Aidan Kavanagh, *Elements of Rite: A Handbook of Liturgical Style* (New York: Pueblo, 1982), 54–55.

2. Paul Turner, *Ages of Initiation*, 39.

3. Rita Ferrone, *Liturgy: Sacrosanctum Concilium*, Rediscovering Vatican II (Mahwah, NJ: Paulist Press, 2007), 18.

4. Ibid., 23–50.

5. Sofia Cavalletti, *The Religious Potential of the Child* (Chicago: Liturgy Training Publications, 1992), 42.

6. Shepard, "What Does It Mean to Be a Child?" 75.

7. See Paul Turner, *Let Us Pray: A Guide to the Rubrics of Sunday Mass* (Collegeville, MN: Liturgical Press, 2006).

8. Christiane Brusselmanns, *We Celebrate the Eucharist,* http://www.rclbenziger.com/Products/S6740/sacrament-preparation---we-celebrate-the-eucharist.aspx (accessed January 1, 2014).

9. See Peter McGrail, *First Communion*, 13, 22, 34.

10. See Anne Y. Koester, *Sunday Mass: Our Role and Why It Matters* (Collegeville, MN: Liturgical Press, 2007), 15.

11. Shepard, "What Does It Mean to Be a Child?" 76.

Epilogue—pages 88–90

1. See the various responses to "The Celebration of First Communion and the Eclipse of Liturgical Principles," Praytellblog .com. May 6, 2013.

2. Huebner, "Religious Metaphors in the Language of Education," in *The Lure of the Transcendent*, 360.

Bibliography

Liturgies

Rite of Baptism for Children. In *The Rites of the Catholic Church.* Collegeville, MN: Liturgical Press, 1990. 1:359–466.

Rite of Christian Initiation of Adults. In *The Rites of the Catholic Church.* Collegeville, MN: Liturgical Press, 1990. 1:15–356.

Documents

Catechism of the Catholic Church. 2nd ed. Washington, DC: United States Conference of Catholic Bishops, 2000.

Code of Canon Law. Latin-English Edition. New English Translation. Washington, DC: Canon Law Society of America, 1998.

Francis, Pope. *Lumen Fidei* (The Light of Faith), June 29, 2013.

Pius XII, Pope. On the Sacred Liturgy (*Mediator Dei*), November 20, 1947.

Sacred Congregation for Divine Worship, Directory for Masses with Children (*Pueros Baptizatos*), 1 November 1973. In *Documents on the Liturgy, 1963–1979: Conciliar, Papal, and Curial Texts.* Collegeville, MN: Liturgical Press, 1982. Pp. 676–88.

Sacred Congregation of Rites, Instruction on Eucharistic Worship (*Eucharisticum Mysterium*), May 25, 1967. In *Documents on the Liturgy, 1963–1979: Conciliar, Papal, and Curial Texts.* Collegeville, MN: Liturgical Press, 1982. 179. Pp. 395–420.

United States Catholic Conference. *Guidelines for the Celebration of the Sacraments with Persons with Disabilities.* Washington, DC: United States Catholic Conference, 1995.

————. *Our Hearts Were Burning Within Us: A Pastoral Plan for Adult Faith Formation in the United States.* Washington, DC: United States Catholic Conference, 1999.

United States Conference of Catholic Bishops. *National Directory for Catechesis.* Washington, DC: United States Conference of Catholic Bishops, 2005.

————. *Sing to the Lord: Music in Catholic Worship.* Washington, DC: United States Conference of Catholic Bishops, 2007.

Vatican II Council, Constitution on the Sacred Liturgy (*Sacrosanctum Concilium*), December 4, 1963. In *Vatican Council II: The Conciliar and Postconciliar Documents.* Translated by Austin Flannery. Collegeville, MN: Liturgical Press, 2014. Pp. 1–36.

Vatican II Council, Dogmatic Constitution on the Church (*Lumen Gentium*), November 21, 1964. In *Vatican Council II: The Conciliar and Postconciliar Documents.* Translated by Austin Flannery. Collegeville, MN: Liturgical Press, 2014. Pp. 350–426.

Secondary Sources

Beal, John P., James A. Coriden, Thomas J. Green, eds. *The New Commentary on the Code of Canon Law: Commissioned by the Canon Law Society of America.* Mahwah, NJ: Paulist Press, 2000.

Brueggemann, Walter. *The Prophetic Imagination.* 2nd ed. Minneapolis: Fortress, 2001.

Brusselmans, Christiane and Brian A. Haggerty. *We Celebrate the Eucharist.* RCL Benziger Publishing, Cincinnati, OH. http://www.rclbenziger.com/Products/S6740/sacrament-preparation---we-celebrate-the-eucharist.aspx (accessed January 1, 2014.

Cavalletti, Sofia. *The Religious Potential of the Child.* Chicago: Liturgy Training Publications, 1992.

Collins, Mary. "Is the Adult Church Ready for Liturgy with Young Christians?" In *The Sacred Play of Children.* Edited by Diane Apostolos-Cappadona. New York: Seabury, 1983.

Condon, Diane. "Faith First at Home—A Family Tradition," *Ag-neWs,* Spring 2004.

Cote, Richard. *Lazarus! Come Out! Why Faith Needs Imagination.* Ottawa: Novalis, 2003.

Crotty, Matthew M. *The Recipient of First Holy Communion: A Historical Synopsis and Commentary.* Washington, DC: Catholic University of America Press, 1947.

Dougherty, Joseph. *From Altar-Throne to Table: The Campaign for Frequent Holy Communion in the Catholic Church.* Lanham, MD: The Scarecrow Press, 2010.

Egeria. *Egeria's Travels.* Translated by John Wilkinson. Warminster, England: Aris & Phillips, 1999.

Eschenauer, Donna M. "The Celebration of First Communion and the Eclipse of Liturgical Principles." Praytellblog.com, May 6, 2013.

———. *The Easter Triduum: A Ritual Pilgrimage.* San Jose, CA: Resource Publications, 2013.

———. "A Second Look at the *Directory for Masses with Children.*" Praytellblog.com, September 3, 2010.

Faggioli, Massimo. *True Reform: Liturgy and Ecclesiology in* Sacrosanctum Concilium. Collegeville, MN: Liturgical Press, 2012.

Ferrone, Rita. *Liturgy: Sacrosanctum Concilium.* Rediscovering Vatican II. Mahwah, NJ: Paulist Press, 2007.

Franklin, R. W., and Robert L. Spaeth. *Virgil Michel American Catholic.* Collegeville, MN: Liturgical Press, 1988.

Groome, Thomas. *Will There Be Faith: A New Vision for Educating and Growing Disciples.* New York: HarperCollins, 2011.

Harris, Maria. *Fashion Me A People: Curriculum in the Church.* Louisville, KY: Westminster John Knox, 1989.

———. *Teaching and the Religious Imagination: An Essay in the Theology of Teaching.* San Francisco: HarperCollins, 1987.

Herr, William A. *This Our Church (Basics of Christian Thought)* Chicago: The Thomas More Press, 1986.

Hudock, Barry. *The Eucharistic Prayer: A User's Guide.* Collegeville, MN: Liturgical Press, 2010.

Huebner, Dwayne. "The Capacity for Wonder and Education." In *The Lure of the Transcendent: Collected Essays by Dwayne Huebner,* edited by Vikki Hillis, 1–10. Mahwah, NJ: Lawrence Erlbaum Associates, Publishers, 1999.

————. "Religious Metaphors in the Language of Education." In *The Lure of the Transcendent: Collected Essays by Dwayne Huebner,* edited by Vikki Hillis, 358–68. Mahwah, NJ: Lawrence Erlbaum Associates, Publishers, 1999.

Irwin, Kevin W. *Models of the Eucharist.* Mahwah, NJ: Paulist Press, 2005.

Johnson, Maxwell E. *The Rites of Christian Initiation: Their Evolution and Interpretation.* Collegeville, MN: Liturgical Press, 2007.

Kavanagh, Aidan. *Elements of Rite: A Handbook of Liturgical Style.* New York: Pueblo, 1982.

————. *The Shape of Baptism: The Rite of Christian Initiation.* New York: Pueblo, 1978.

Koester, Anne Y. *Sunday Mass: Our Role and Why It Matters.* Collegeville, MN: Liturgical Press, 2007.

Laurance, John D. *The Sacrament of the Eucharist.* Lex Orandi. Collegeville, MN: Liturgical Press, 2012.

Martini, Teri. *The Fisherman's Ring: The Life of Saint Pius X, The Children's Pope.* Patterson, NJ: St. Anthony Guild, 1954.

Marx, OSB, Paul B. *Virgil Michel and the Liturgical Movement.* Collegeville, MN: Liturgical Press, 1957.

Mazza, Enrico. *Mystagogy: A Theology of Liturgy in the Patristic Age.* Translated by Matthew J. O'Connell. New York: Pueblo, 1989.

McGrail, Peter. *First Communion: Ritual, Church and Popular Religious Identity.* Burlington, VT: Ashgate, 2007.

Metzdorff, Jo-Ann. "The Consumer Culture and Family Faith Formation, Practice and Preparation for First Holy Communion." DMin diss., Seminary of the Immaculate Conception, 2007.

Mitchell, Nathan. *Meeting Mystery: Liturgy, Worship, Sacraments.* Theology in Global Perspectives. Maryknoll, NY: Orbis, 2006.

Moran, Gabriel. *Education Towards Adulthood: Religion and Lifelong Learning.* New York: Paulist Press, 1979.

————. *Religious Education Development: Images for the Future.* Minneapolis: Winston, 1983.

————. *Religious Education as a Second Language.* Birmingham, AL: Religious Education Press, 1989.

————. *Showing How: The Act of Teaching.* Valley Forge, PA: Trinity Press International, 1997.

O'Malley, John W. *Trent: What Happened at the Council.* Cambridge, MA: Belknap, 2013.

Ostdiek, Gilbert. *Catechesis for Liturgy: A Program for Parish Involvement.* Washington, DC: Pastoral Press, 1986.

Pecklers, Keith F. *The Unread Vision: The Liturgical Movement in the United States of America, 1926–1955.* Collegeville, MN: Liturgical Press, 1998.

Pius X, Pope. *All Things in Christ: Encyclicals and Selected Documents of Saint Pius X.* Translated by Vincent A. Yzermans. Westminster, MD: The Newman Press, 1954.

————. *Catechetical Documents of Pope Pius X.* Edited and translated by Joseph B. Collins. Paterson, NJ: Saint Anthony Guild, 1946.

Rahner, Karl. *The Content of Faith: The Best of Karl Rahner's Theological Writings.* Edited by Karl Lehmann and Albert Raffelt. New York: Crossroads, 1992.

Ratzinger, Joseph Cardinal. *God Is Near Us: The Eucharist the Heart of Life.* San Francisco: Ignatius, 2003.

Rizzo, David. *Faith, Family, and Children with Special Needs: How Catholic Parents and Their Kids with Special Needs Can Develop a Richer Spiritual Life.* Chicago: Loyola, 2012.

Saint-Exupéry, Antoine de. *The Little Prince.* Translated by Richard Howard. New York: Harcourt Brace, 1943.

Scott, Kieran. "Continuity and Change in Religious Education." In *Critical Issues in Religious Education,* edited by Oliver Brennan. Dublin, Ireland: Veritas, 2005.

Searle, Mark. "Children in the Assembly of the Church." In *Children in the Assembly of the Church,* edited by Eleanor Bernstein and John Brooks-Leonard. Chicago: Liturgy Training Publications, 1992.

————. *The Church Speaks About Sacraments With Children: Baptism, Confirmation, Eucharist, Penance.* Chicago: Liturgy Training Publications, 1990.

————. "Images and Worship." In *Vision: The Scholarly Contributions of Mark Searle to Liturgical Renewal,* edited by Anne Y. Koester and Barbara Searle. Collegeville, MN: Liturgical Press, 2004.

Senn, Frank C. *Christian Liturgy: Catholic and Evangelical.* Minneapolis: Fortress, 1997.

Shepard, Thomas. "What Does It Mean to Be a Child?" In *Children, Liturgy and Music,* edited by Virgil C. Funk. Washington, DC: The Pastoral Press, 1990.

Taft, Robert. *Beyond East and West: Problems in Liturgical Understanding.* Rome, Italy: Pontifico Istituto Orientale, 2001.

Turner, Paul. *Ages of Initiation: The First Two Christian Millennia.* Collegeville, MN: Liturgical Press, 2000.

————. *The Hallelujah Highway: A History of the Catechumenate.* Chicago: Liturgy Training Publications, 2000.

————. *Let Us Pray: A Guide to the Rubrics of Sunday Mass.* Collegeville, MN: Liturgical Press, 2006.

Upton, Julia. *A Church for the Next Generation: Sacraments in Transition.* Collegeville, MN: Liturgical Press, 1990.

————. "Personal Obstacles to Ritual Prayer." In *The Renewal That Awaits Us*, edited by Eleanor Bernstein and Martin F. Connell. Chicago: Liturgy Training Publications, 1997.

Yarnold, Edward. *The Awe-Inspiring Rites of Initiation: The Origins of the R.C.I.A.* Collegeville, MN: Liturgical Press, 1994.